DAWN 4
AWAKE MY SOUL 7
COME ALIVE 23
SEE THE LIGHT 41
NO ONE BUT YOU 54
KING OF KINGS 70
I WILL PRAISE YOU 85
FROM WHOM ALL BLESSINGS FLOW (DOXOLOGY) 97
EVERY BREATH 110
BRIGHT AS THE SUN 123
UPPER ROOM 141
HE SHALL REIGN 150

HILLSONG WORSHIP

Hillsong Worship is the legacy worship expression of Hillsong Church, representing the strength and generations of our global worship team. Hillsong Worship exists to serve the global Church and equip believers everywhere with songs of Holy Spirit power that exalt and glorify the Name of Jesus, build the Church and fuel revival on the earth.

UNITED, Y&F AND HILLSONG KIDS TEAMS

UNITED is committed to writing songs that speak truth, create a unique sound, connect with churches, individuals and ultimately connect people everywhere with God. Young & Free (Y&F) is the creative worship expression of Hillsong Church's current youth movement. When on tour, both UNITED and Young & Free are accompanied by the whole Hillsong team's support and prayers that their ministry would arrest hearts and point people to Jesus, impacting individuals, local youth groups and local churches. UNITED and Y&F teams also serve as part of Hillsong Worship and our worship and creative team. HILLSONG KIDS is the children's ministry of Hillsong Church, creating moments kids will never forget as they grow in faith through Christ Jesus.

WE ARE A CHURCH COMMITTED TO INSPIRING AND EMPOWERING THE AUTHENTIC WORSHIP OF JESUS AND RESOURCING THE BODY OF CHRIST.

There are numerous resources we as Hillsong make available including inspiring teaching and books by Brian & Bobbie Houston, curriculum content that can impact your childrens, outreach and discipleship ministries and of course music. For more information visit hillsongmusic.com

WE ARE A CHURCH THAT BELIEVES IN CHAMPIONING THE CAUSE OF THE LOCAL CHURCH.

Hillsong Conference is about you, your church and seeing God's Kingdom advance across the earth. This is your chance to lean in, receive and take home practical teachings you can outwork in your own church home, family and community. It's about being refreshed and inspired and finding great strength and unity amongst the diversity of the local church worldwide. For more information visit hillsong.com/conference

WE ARE A CHURCH THAT BELIEVES IN PLACING VALUE UPON WOMANHOOD.

Colour Conference at the very core is a strong humanitarian message. Our passion and labour is to place value upon womanhood, so that we in turn can arise from a place of strength and cohesion and place value upon fellow humanity. For more information visit hillsong.com/colour

WE ARE A CHURCH THAT BELIEVES IN REACHING AND INFLUENCING THE WORLD WITH THE MESSAGE OF JESUS CHRIST.

Hillsong Channel is an innovative media movement, beaming the timeless message of JESUS around the globe into television screens and digital devices to empower people in every sphere of life. This is a platform positioned in the heart of culture bringing JESUS into prisons and palaces all over the world. For more information visit hillsong.com/channel

Hillsong Television with Brian Houston is a half-hour Christian television program that features his teaching from Hillsong Church services. Pastor Brian's messages are empowering, passionate and practical for everyday life. His teaching will inspire you with the hope, joy, meaning and purpose that can be found in a personal and loving God. For more information visit hillsong.com/tv

WE ARE A CHURCH THAT BELIEVES IN PARTNERSHIP AND UNITY AS WE ADVANCE HIS KINGDOM ON EARTH.

The Hillsong Leadership Network is all about connecting, equipping and serving leaders and exists to champion the cause of local churches everywhere. Our heart is that by coming alongside leaders, churches and ministries of varying denominations and styles, we are able to see more churches flourish and reach their God-given potential through this membership program. For more information visit hillsong.com/network

WE ARE A CHURCH THAT BELIEVES IN EQUIPPING PEOPLE WITH PRINCIPLES AND TOOLS TO LEAD AND IMPACT IN EVERY SPHERE OF LIFE.

To find further information about the Pastoral Leadership Streams (including Youth, Children, Event Management, or Social Justice Pathways), Creative Streams (including Worship Music, TV & Media, Dance and Production) or a Degree Program offered on campus by Alphacrucis College visit hillsong.com/college

WE ARE A CHURCH IN MANY LOCATIONS:

AFRICA: Kenya, Mauritius, South Africa ASIA PACIFIC: Australia, Indonesia EUROPE: Denmark, France, Germany, Italy, Netherlands, Norway, Portugal, Russia, Spain, Sweden, Switzerland, Ukraine, United Kingdom LATIN AMERICA: Argentina, Brazil, Mexico, Uruguay MIDDLE EAST: Israel NORTH AMERICA: Canada, USA ONLINE: Online Campus, Church of the Air. For service times and information visit hillsong.com

OUR PRAYER

Our prayer is that you would discover the Author of love… the Lord Jesus Christ. His life and death represent the greatest gift of love the world will ever see… "This is real love – not that we loved God, but that He loved us and sent His Son as a sacrifice to take away our sins." (1 John 4:10 NLT) God paid the ultimate sacrifice sending His Son, Jesus Christ, who died on the cross in our place and rose again to prove His victory, restore us to relationship with Him and empower us for life. It is through Jesus Christ that we can know and be reconciled with God… all we need to do is believe in Him and accept Jesus Christ as our Lord and Saviour. It is as simple as praying a prayer… asking Jesus to meet you right where you are… it is a brand new start of living in relationship with God… if you are not sure that you personally know the Lord Jesus, we would like to encourage you to make this your prayer today:

Dear Lord Jesus, thank You for dying on the cross for me. Thank You for Your amazing love. I repent of my sins and thank You for Your forgiveness. Please come into my life and give me a fresh start. I believe in You and accept You as my Lord and Saviour. I am now a Christian – a follower of Jesus Christ and You now live in me. Help me to live my life for You from this day forward. Amen.

If you have prayed this prayer today, we would love to hear from you! Please write to us at: Hillsong Church, PO Box 1195, Castle Hill, NSW 1765, Australia or email us at: prayer@hillsong.com

TERMS AND CONDITIONS

Thank you for purchasing sheet music from Hillsong Music. Your purchase grants you the right to make ONE copy of the sheet music for your personal purposes (performances, worship services, personal study, musical teaching, etc). However the following rights have NOT been granted to you:
1. Reproduce copies of the sheet music in whole or in part outside of the rights granted to you above.
2. To translate, enhance, modify, alter or adapt the sheet music or any part of it for any purpose.
3. Cause or permit any third party to translate, enhance, modify, alter or adapt the sheet music or any part of it for any purpose.
4. Sub-licence, lease, lend, sell, rent, distribute or grant others any rights, or provide copies of the sheet music to others. Reproductions of the sheet music can be made for the purpose of church worship only with an existing Music Reproduction Licence from CCLI. For further information contact CCLI at http://www.ccli.com

For further information about copyright or other use of this music, please contact Hillsong Music Publishing at publishing@hillsong.com

TRANSCRIBED AND ENGRAVED BY JARED HASCHEK & DANIEL HERNANDEZ

DAWN

Music by
BROOKE LIGERTWOOD

© 2019 Hillsong Music Publishing Australia.
All rights reserved. International copyright secured. Used by permission.
Tel: +61 2 8853 5284 Email: publishing@hillsong.com

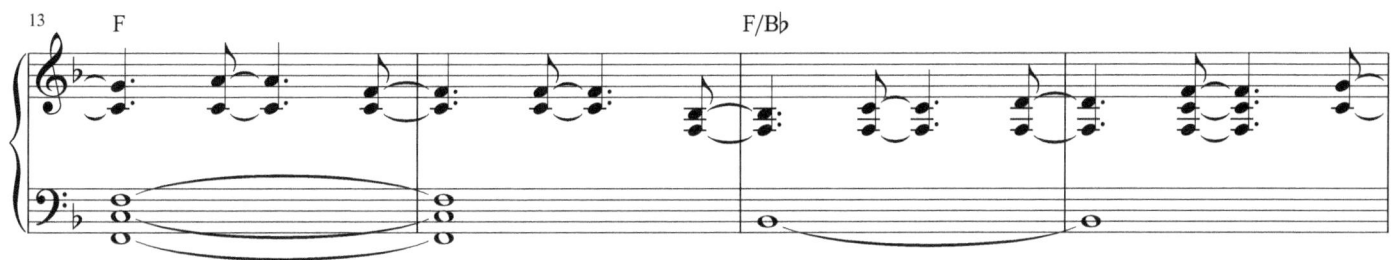
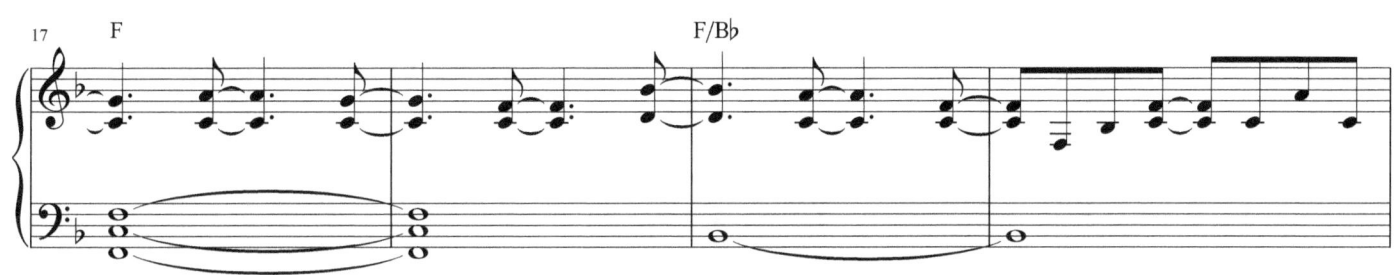

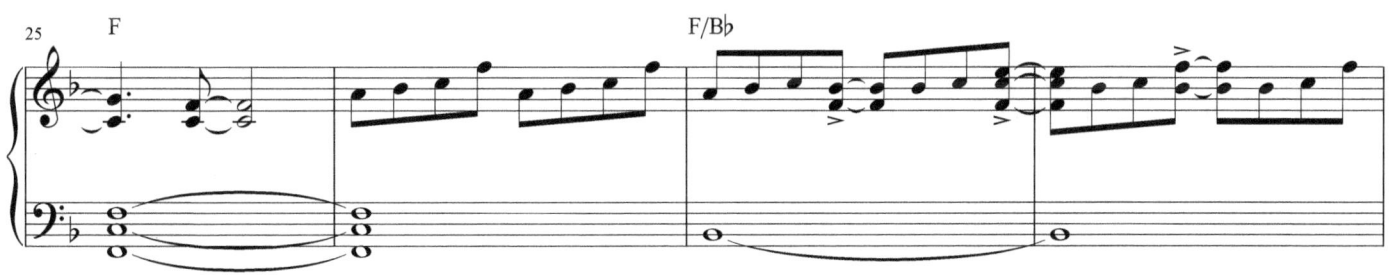

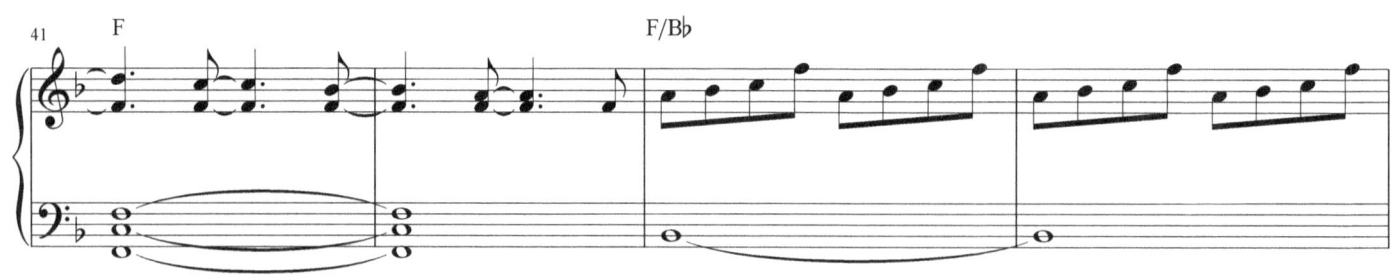

Segue as one to Awake My Soul

AWAKE MY SOUL

Words and Music by
BROOKE LIGERTWOOD

© 2019 Hillsong Music Publishing Australia.
All rights reserved. International copyright secured. Used by permission.
Tel: +61 2 8853 5284 Email: publishing@hillsong.com CCLI Song No. 7134998

There is a sound that chang - es things, the sound of His peo -

AWAKE MY SOUL

Words and Music by
BROOKE LIGERTWOOD

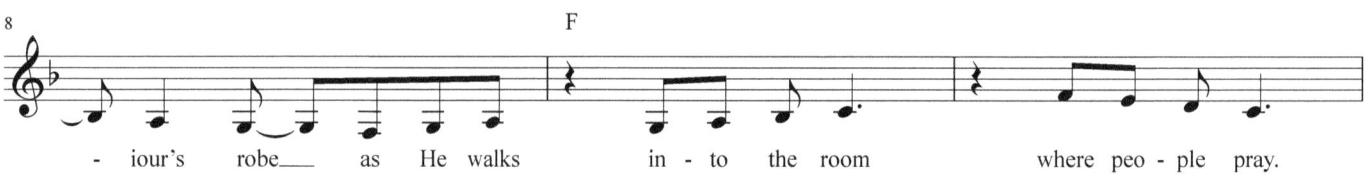

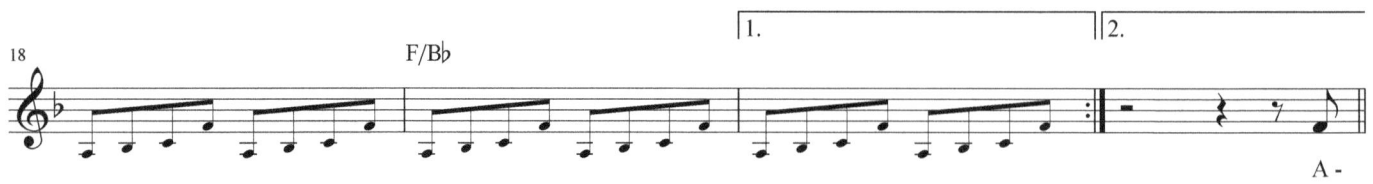

© 2019 Hillsong Music Publishing Australia.
All rights reserved. International copyright secured. Used by permission.
Tel: +61 2 8853 5284 Email: publishing@hillsong.com CCLI Song No. 7134998

AWAKE MY SOUL

**Words and Music by
Brooke Ligertwood**

VERSE 1:
There is a sound I love to hear
It's the sound of the Saviour's robe
As He walks into the room where people pray
Where we hear praises He hears faith

VERSE 2:
There is a sound I love to hear
It's the sound of the Saviour's robe
As He walks into the room where people pray
Where we hear worship He hears faith

CHORUS:
Awake my soul and sing
Sing His praise aloud
Sing His praise aloud

© 2019 Hillsong Music Publishing Australia
CCLI: 7134998

PO Box 1195 Castle Hill NSW 1765
Ph: +61 2 8853 5284 Fx: +61 2 8846 4625
E-mail: publishing@hillsong.com

VERSE 3:
There is a sound that changes things
The sound of His people on their knees
Oh wake up you slumbering
It's time to worship Him

BRIDGE:
And when He moves
And when we pray
Where stood a wall now stands a way
Where every promise is amen

And when He moves
Make no mistake
The bowels of hell begin to shake
All hail the Lord all hail the King

© 2019 Hillsong Music Publishing Australia
CCLI: 7134998

PO Box 1195 Castle Hill NSW 1765
Ph: +61 2 8853 5284 Fx: +61 2 8846 4625
E-mail: publishing@hillsong.com

OPTIONAL AD LIB:
Hey oh
Oh let the King of glory enter in
Hey oh
Fall down on your knees and worship Him
Hey oh
Let His praise rise up don't hold it in

© 2019 Hillsong Music Publishing Australia
CCLI: 7134998

PO Box 1195 Castle Hill NSW 1765
Ph: +61 2 8853 5284 Fx: +61 2 8846 4625
E-mail: publishing@hillsong.com

COME ALIVE

Words and Music by
BENJAMIN HASTINGS, MICHAEL FATKIN
& SCOTT LIGERTWOOD

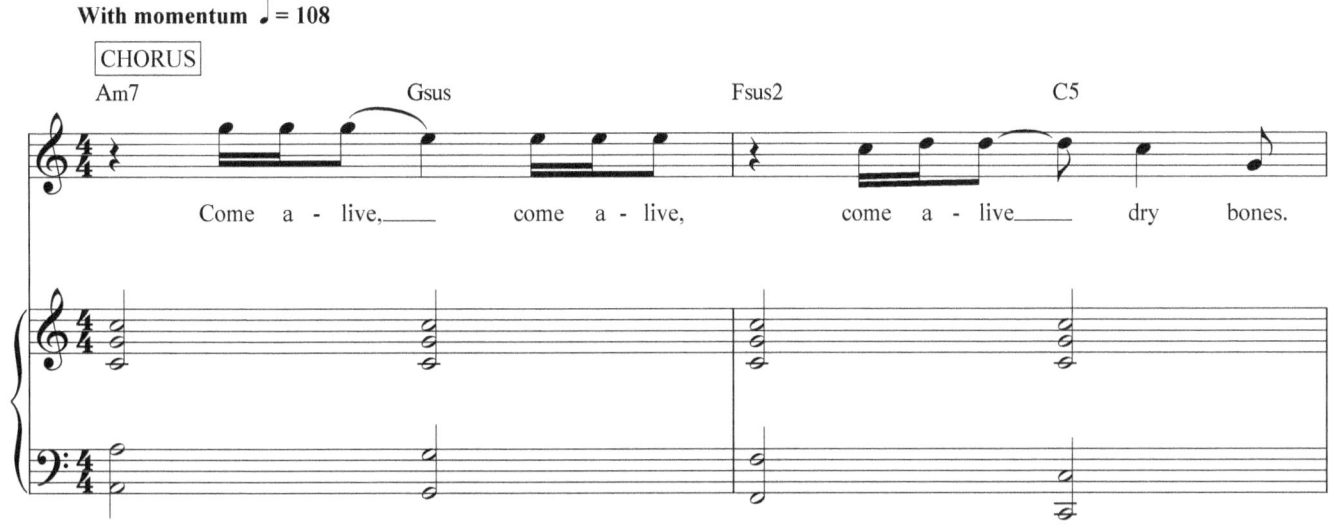

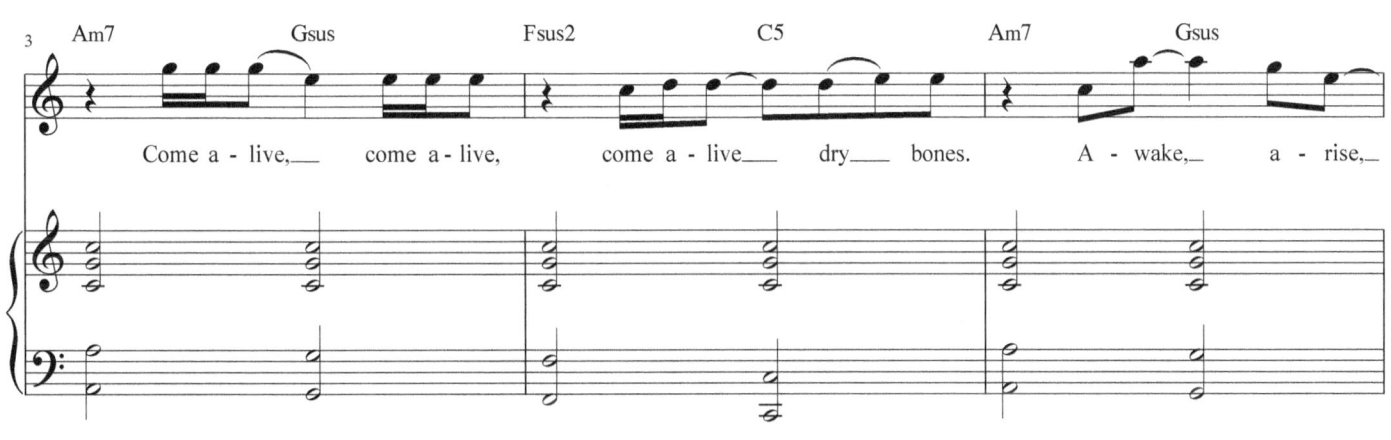

© 2019 Hillsong Music Publishing Australia.
All rights reserved. International copyright secured. Used by permission.
Tel: +61 2 8853 5284 Email: publishing@hillsong.com CCLI Song No. 7134993

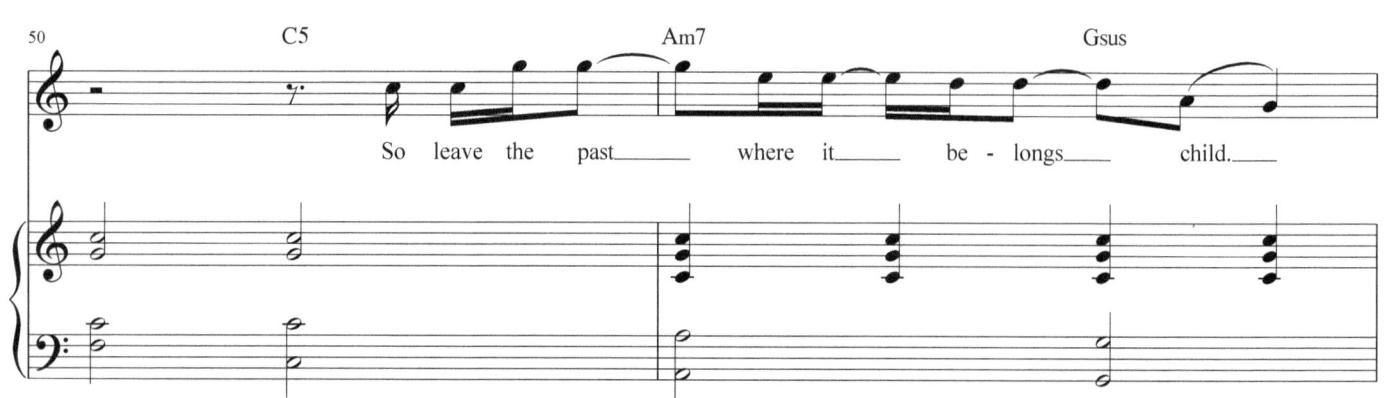

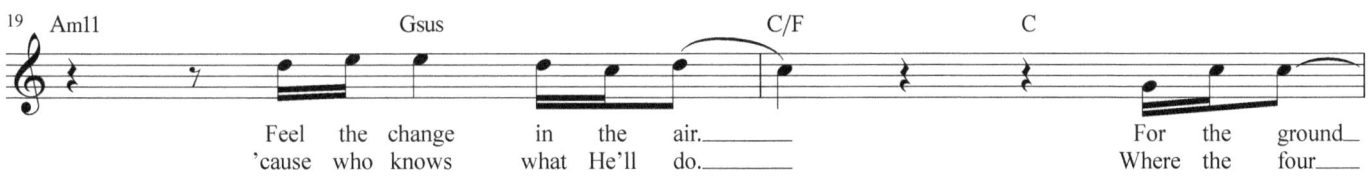

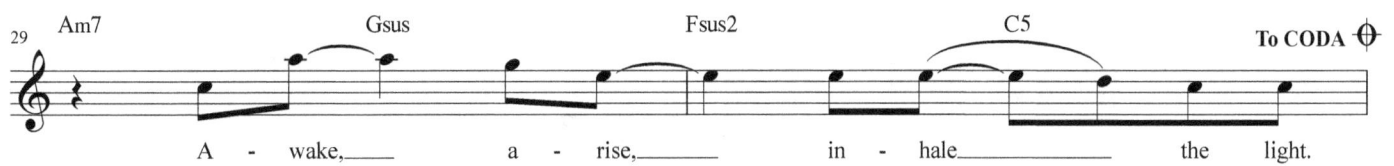

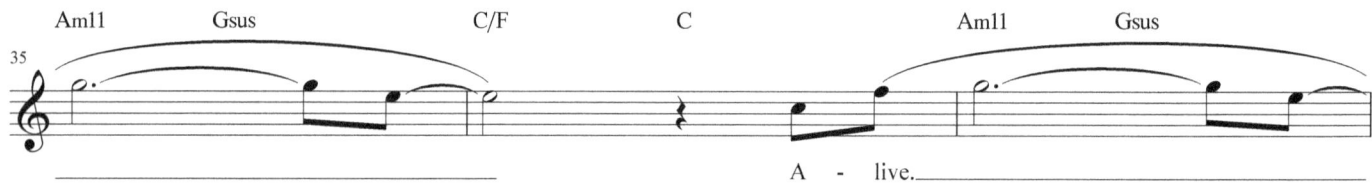
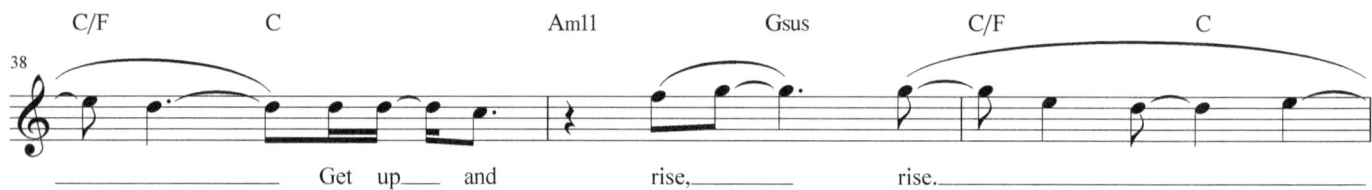
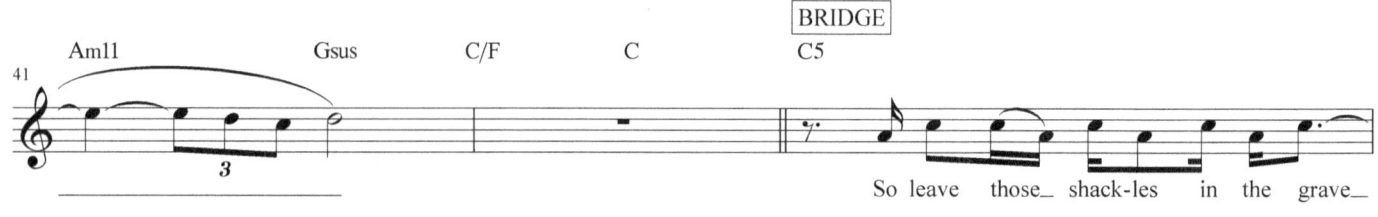
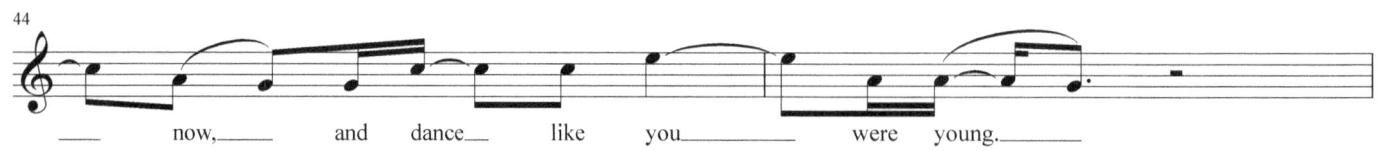

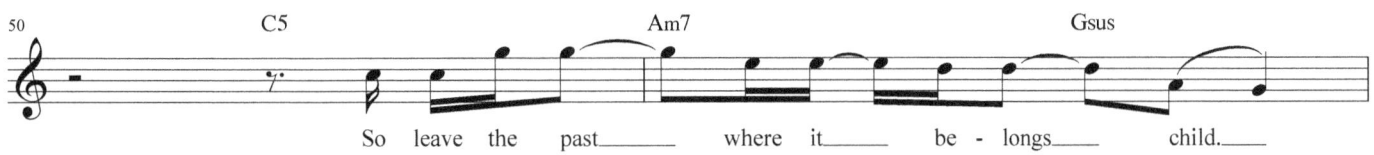
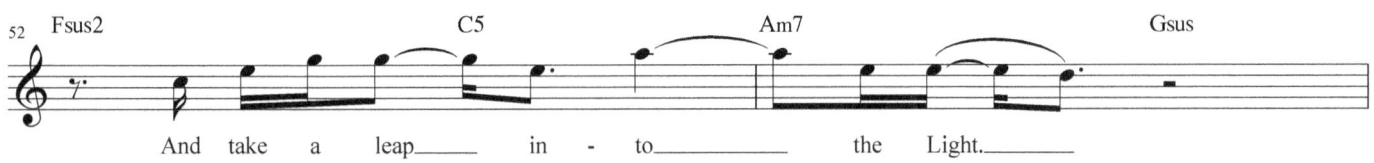
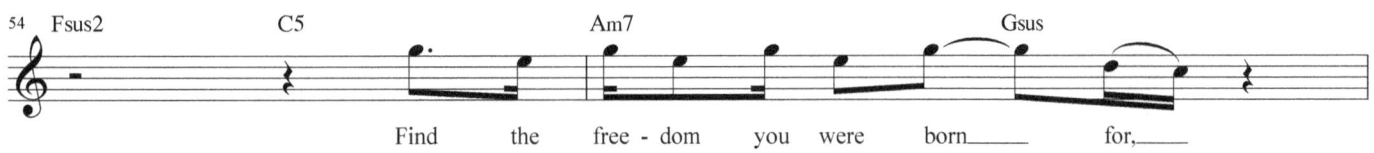

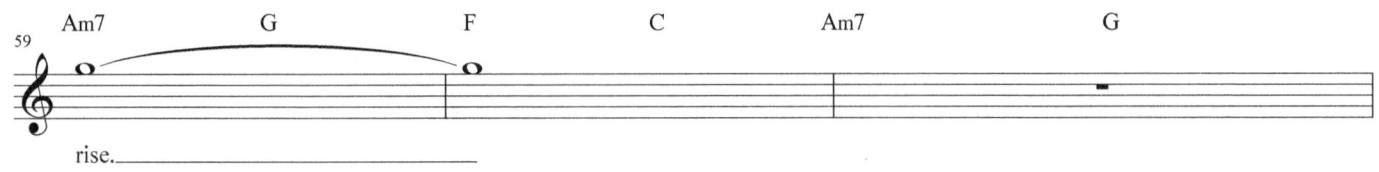
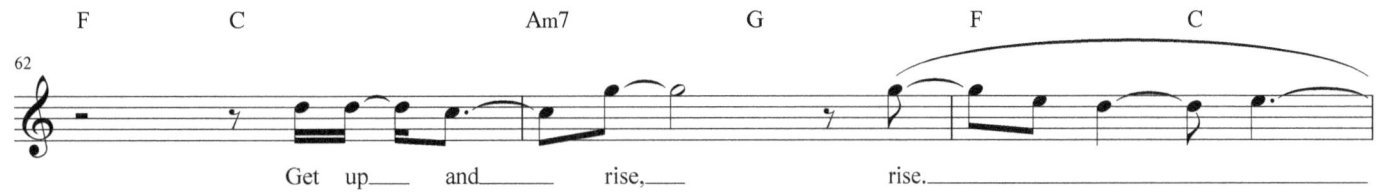

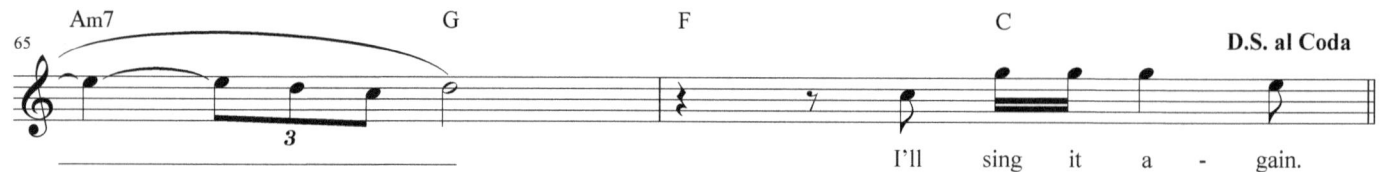

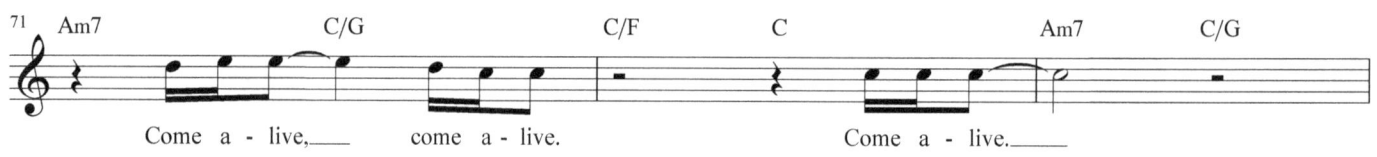
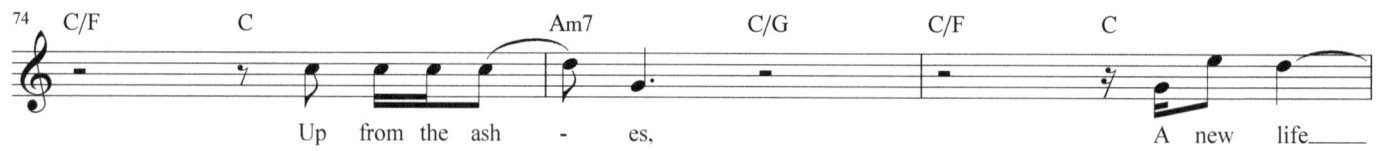

COME ALIVE

**Words and Music by
Benjamin Hastings, Michael Fatkin
& Scott Ligertwood**

CHORUS:
Come alive come alive come alive dry bones
Come alive come alive come alive dry bones
Awake arise
Inhale the light
Come alive come alive

VERSE 1:
I'm gonna sing to you dry bones
Until you're covered in life
And the valley blooms
Like a rosebud in the light

VERSE 2:
Hear the call to attention
Feel the change in the air
For the ground is dry
But the clouds are overhead

© 2019 Hillsong Music Publishing Australia
CCLI: 7134993

PO Box 1195 Castle Hill NSW 1765
Ph: +61 2 8853 5284 Fx: +61 2 8846 4625
E-mail: publishing@hillsong.com

PRE-CHORUS:
I'm gonna sing it again

VERSE 3:
Are you waiting on heaven
Or is it waiting on you
For the Holy Ghost is already in the room

VERSE 4:
So you better get ready
'Cause who knows what He'll do
Where the four winds blow there's a breakthrough breaking through

PRE-CHORUS 2:
I'm gonna prophesy again

POST-CHORUS:
Come alive alive
Get up and rise rise

© 2019 Hillsong Music Publishing Australia
CCLI: 7134993

PO Box 1195 Castle Hill NSW 1765
Ph: +61 2 8853 5284 Fx: +61 2 8846 4625
E-mail: publishing@hillsong.com

BRIDGE:
So leave those shackles in the grave now
And dance like you were young
You do not have to live in chains now
There's a key within your song

So leave the past where it belongs child
And take a leap into the Light
Find the freedom you were born for
And tell that soul to rise
Arise arise arise

Get up and rise rise

I'll sing it again

© 2019 Hillsong Music Publishing Australia
CCLI: 7134993

PO Box 1195 Castle Hill NSW 1765
Ph: +61 2 8853 5284 Fx: +61 2 8846 4625
E-mail: publishing@hillsong.com

POST-CHORUS:
Come alive come alive
Come alive come alive
Come alive

Up from the ashes
A new life is born
Up from the ashes
Flesh on the bone

© 2019 Hillsong Music Publishing Australia
CCLI: 7134993

PO Box 1195 Castle Hill NSW 1765
Ph: +61 2 8853 5284 Fx: +61 2 8846 4625
E-mail: publishing@hillsong.com

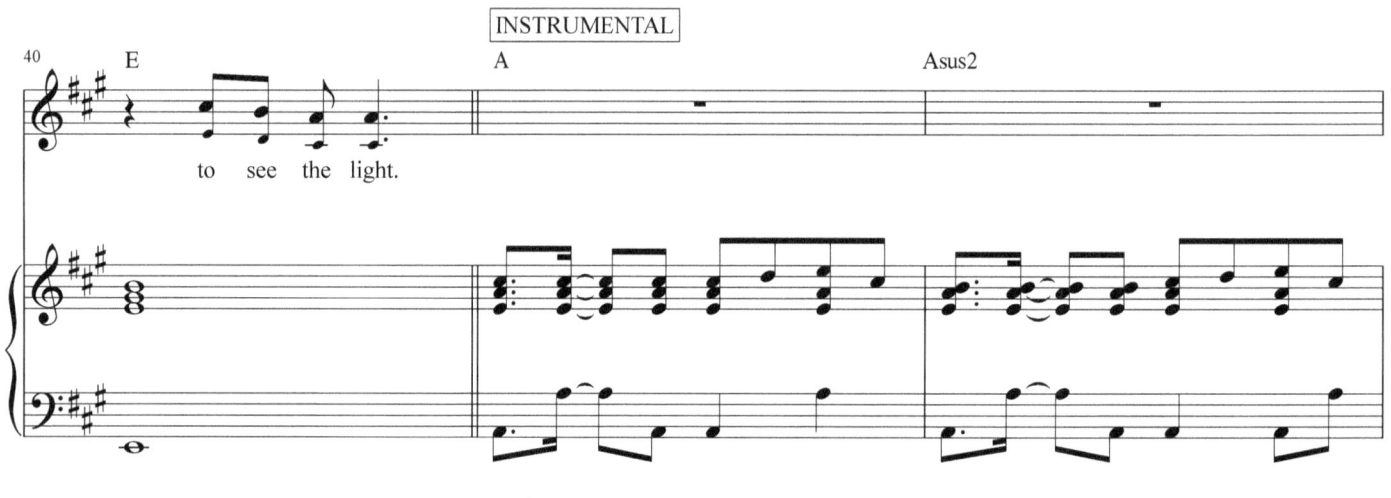

SEE THE LIGHT

Words and Music by
BEN FIELDING & REUBEN MORGAN

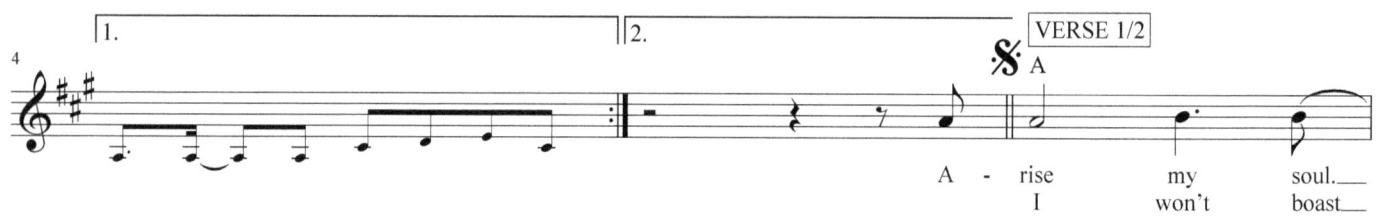
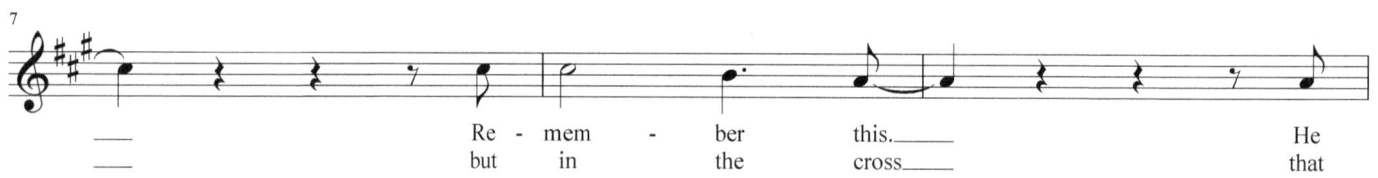

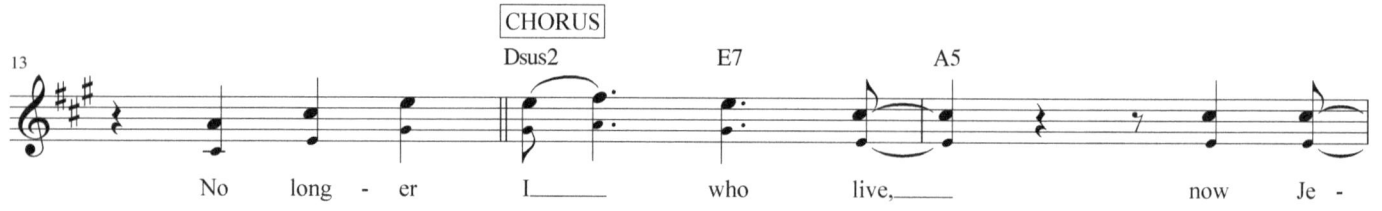
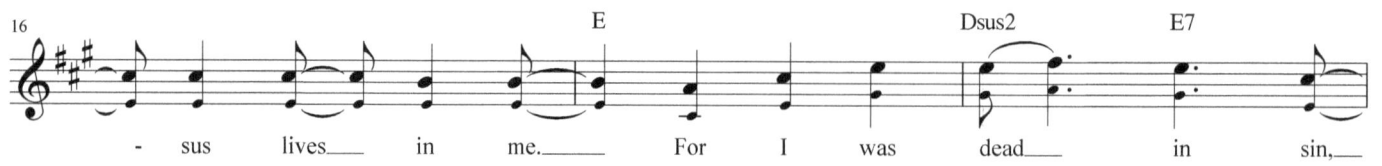

© 2019 Hillsong Music Publishing Australia.
All rights reserved. International copyright secured. Used by permission.
Tel: +61 2 8853 5284 Email: publishing@hillsong.com CCLI Song No. 7134996

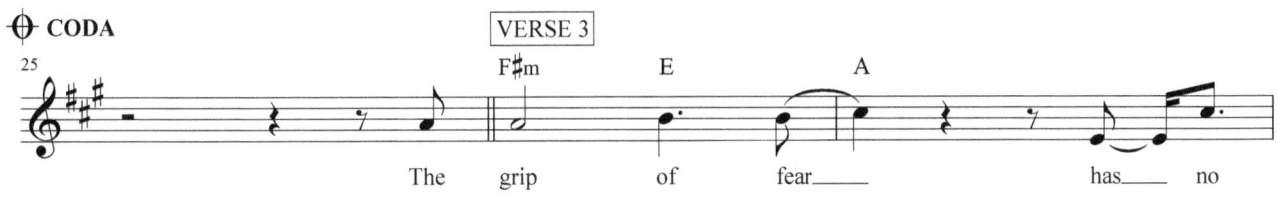

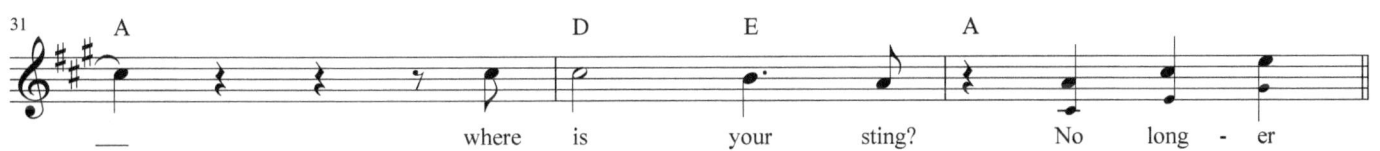

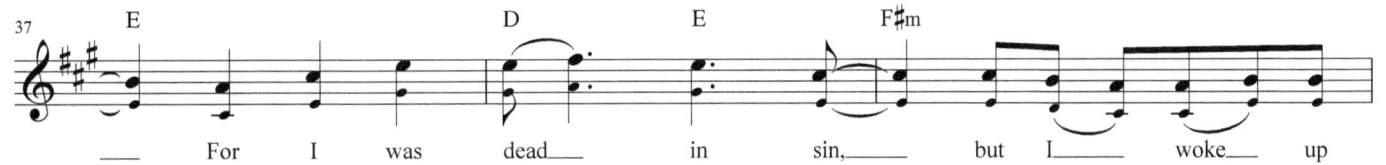

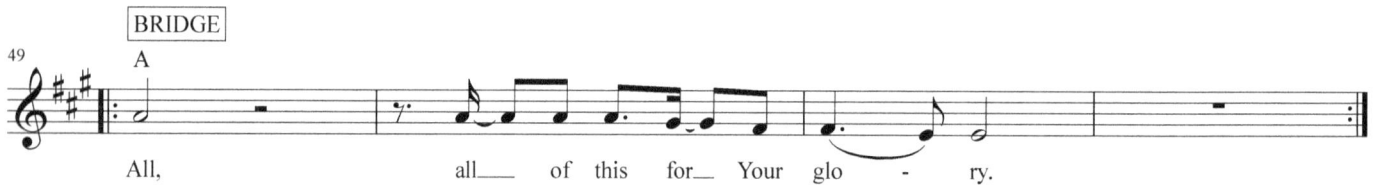

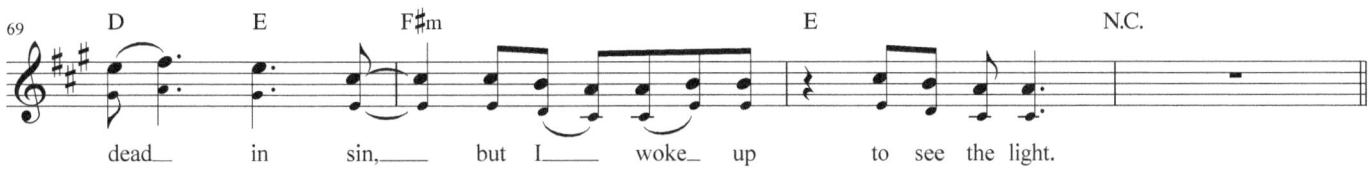

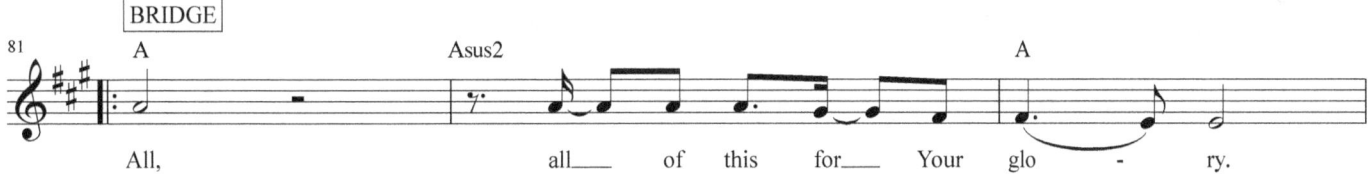

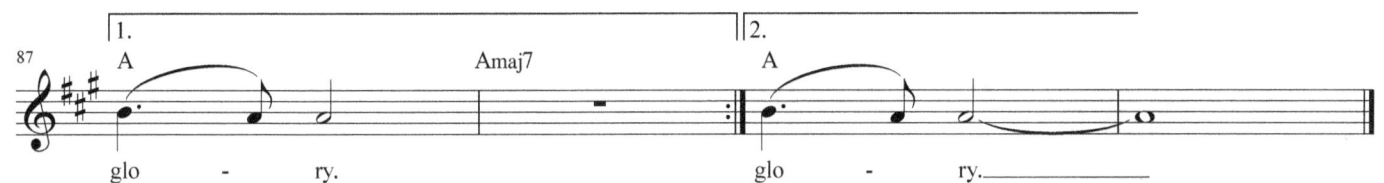

SEE THE LIGHT

**Words and Music by
Ben Fielding & Reuben Morgan**

VERSE 1:
**Arise my soul
Remember this
He took my sin
And He buried it**

CHORUS:
**No longer I who live
Now Jesus lives in me
For I was dead in sin
But I woke up to see the light**

VERSE 2:
**No I won't boast
But in the cross
That saved my soul
All else is loss**

© 2019 Hillsong Music Publishing Australia
CCLI: 7134996

PO Box 1195 Castle Hill NSW 1765
Ph: +61 2 8853 5284 Fx: +61 2 8846 4625
E-mail: publishing@hillsong.com

VERSE 3:
The grip of fear
Has no hold on me
So where o death
Where is your sting

BRIDGE:
All all of this for your glory

© 2019 Hillsong Music Publishing Australia
CCLI: 7134996

PO Box 1195 Castle Hill NSW 1765
Ph: +61 2 8853 5284 Fx: +61 2 8846 4625
E-mail: publishing@hillsong.com

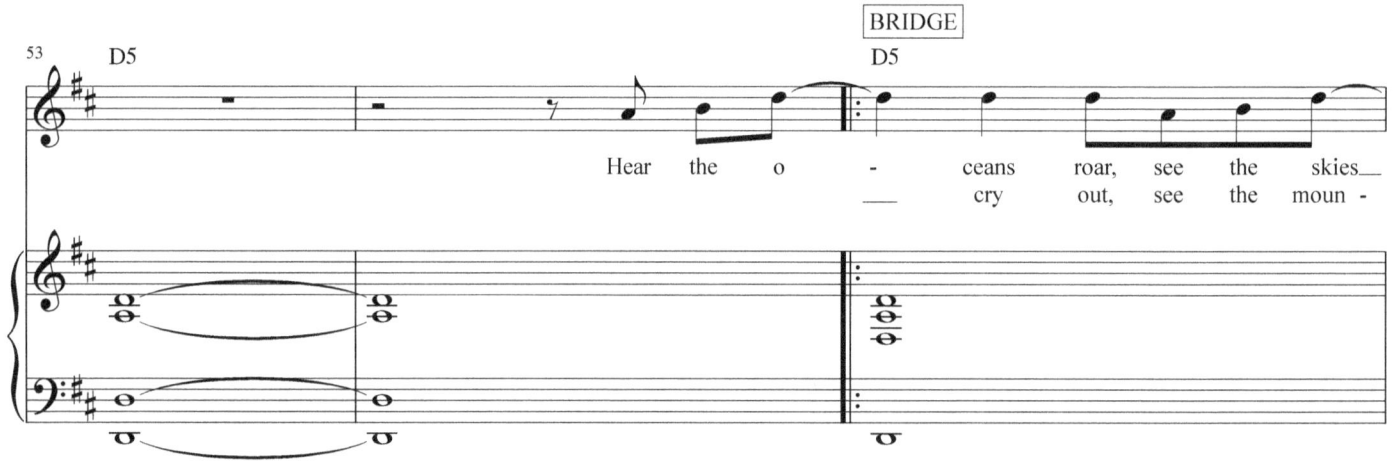
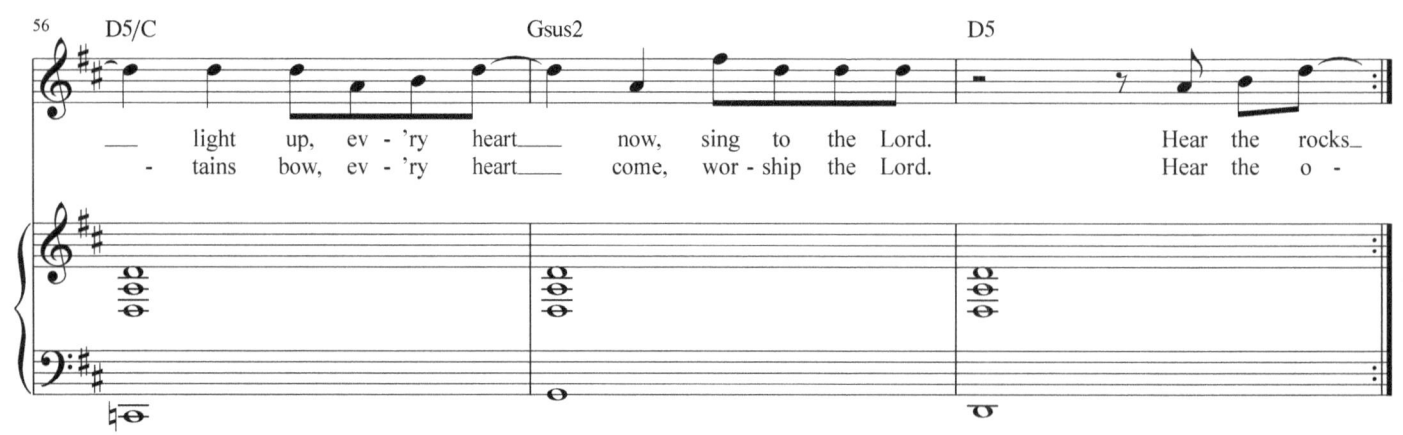

NO ONE BUT YOU

**Words and Music by
SCOTT LIGERTWOOD, AODHAN KING
& BROOKE LIGERTWOOD**

© 2019 Hillsong Music Publishing Australia.
All rights reserved. International copyright secured. Used by permission.
Tel: +61 2 8853 5284 Email: publishing@hillsong.com CCLI Song No. 7135000

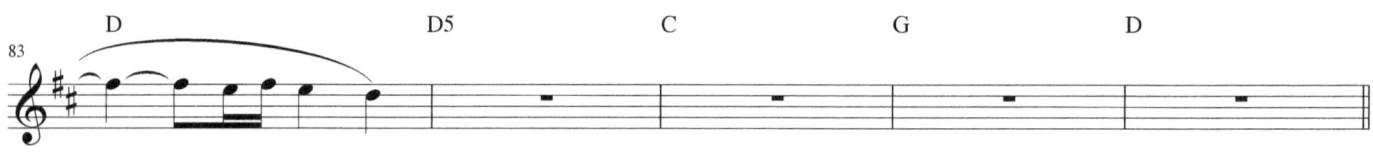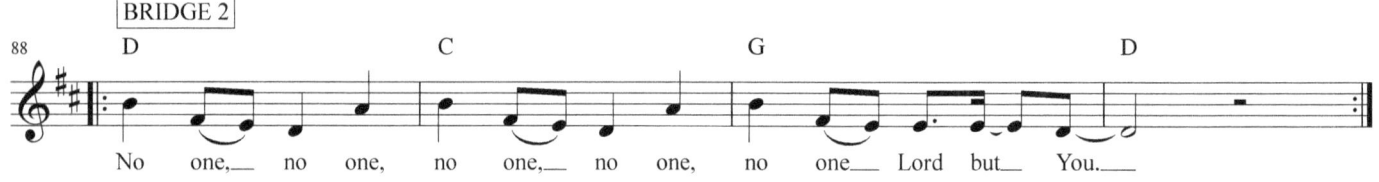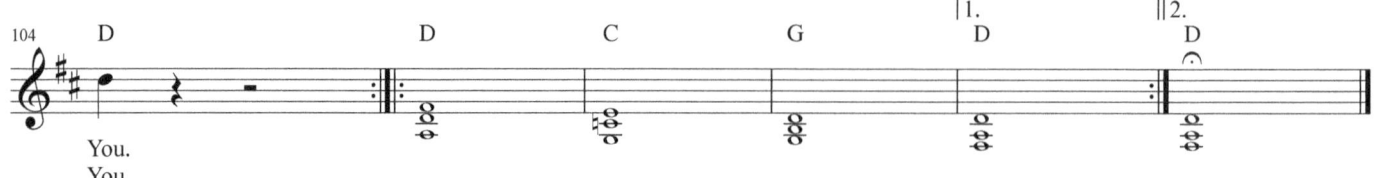

NO ONE BUT YOU

**Words and Music by
Scott Ligertwood, Aodhan King
& Brooke Ligertwood**

VERSE 1:
**Who can melt the hardest heart
And speak life into my soul
Who can spin the world around
And hold me ever close**

VERSE 2:
**Who can search the depths of me
And love me to the core
Who controls the world I see
And walks me through it all**

CHORUS:
**No one but You
No one but You**

© 2019 Hillsong Music Publishing Australia
CCLI: 7135000

PO Box 1195 Castle Hill NSW 1765
Ph: +61 2 8853 5284 Fx: +61 2 8846 4625
E-mail: publishing@hillsong.com

VERSE 3:
Who has made the righteous bright
Who has paved my way with grace
Loved me through my darkest hours
A thousand different ways

POST CHORUS:
I'll sing of Your love
I can't get enough
I just want You

The Lord of my soul
King of my heart
Jesus it's You

BRIDGE:
Hear the oceans roar
See the skies light up
Every heart now
Sing to the Lord

© 2019 Hillsong Music Publishing Australia
CCLI: 7135000

PO Box 1195 Castle Hill NSW 1765
Ph: +61 2 8853 5284 Fx: +61 2 8846 4625
E-mail: publishing@hillsong.com

Hear the rocks cry out
See the mountains bow
Every heart come
Worship the Lord

BRIDGE 2:
No one no one
No one no one
No one Lord but You

© 2019 Hillsong Music Publishing Australia
CCLI: 7135000

PO Box 1195 Castle Hill NSW 1765
Ph: +61 2 8853 5284 Fx: +61 2 8846 4625
E-mail: publishing@hillsong.com

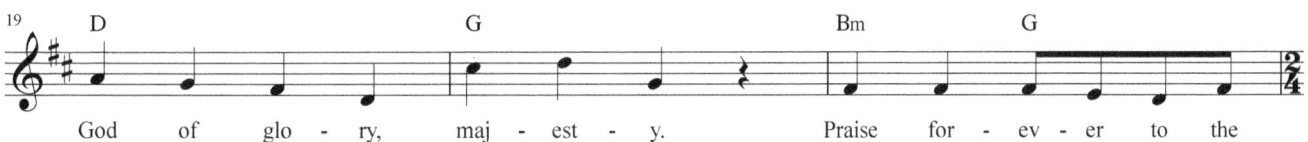

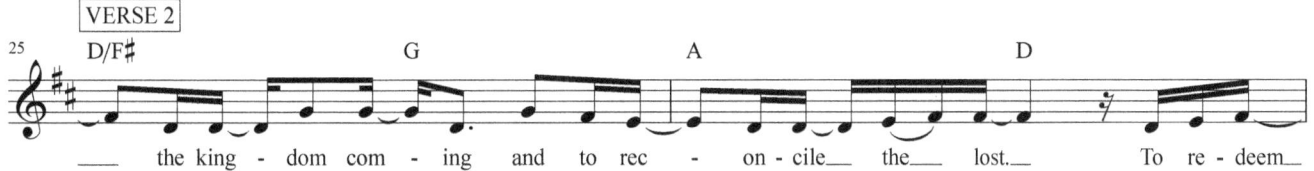
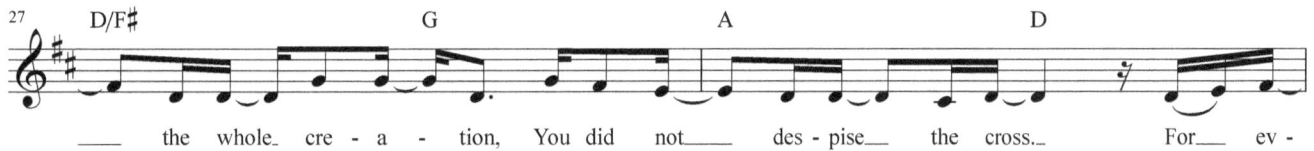

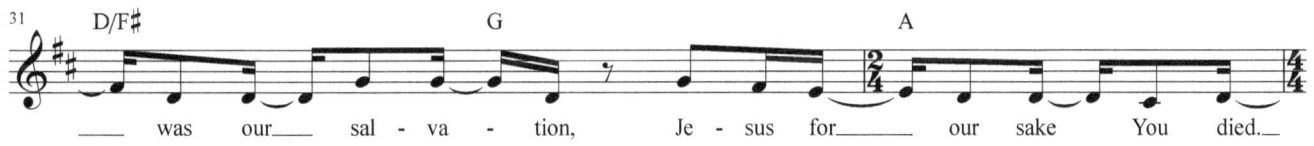

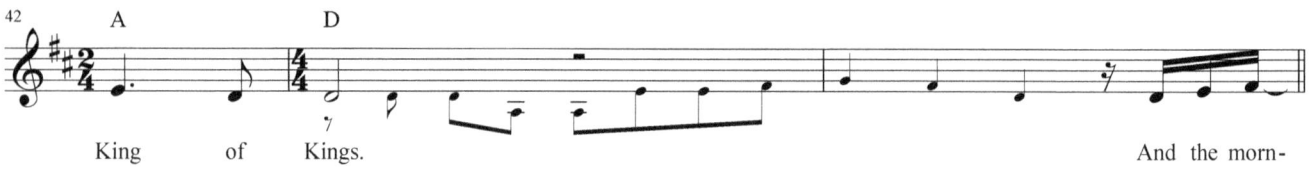

VERSE 3

VERSE 4

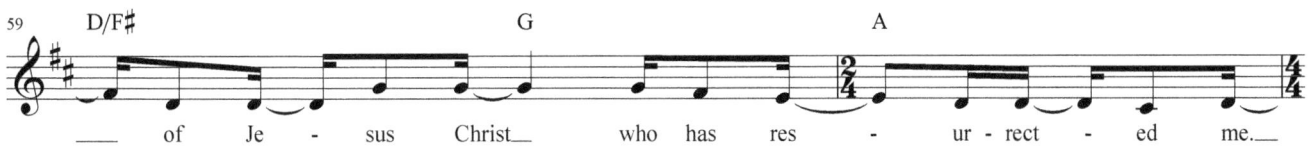

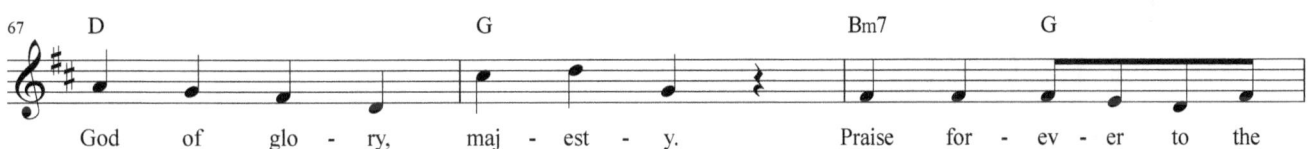

KING OF KINGS

**Words and Music by
Brooke Ligertwood, Scott Ligertwood
& Jason Ingram**

VERSE 1:
In the darkness we were waiting
Without hope without light
Till from heaven You came running
There was mercy in Your eyes

To fulfil the law and prophets
To a virgin came the Word
From a throne of endless glory
To a cradle in the dirt

CHORUS:
Praise the Father
Praise the Son
Praise the Spirit three in one
God of glory
Majesty
Praise forever to the King of Kings

© 2019 Hillsong Music Publishing Australia & Fellow Ships
Music/So Essential Tunes (admin at
EssentialMusicPublishing.com)
CCLI: 7127647

PO Box 1195 Castle Hill NSW 1765
Ph: +61 2 8853 5284 Fx: +61 2 8846 4625
E-mail: publishing@hillsong.com

VERSE 2:
To reveal the kingdom coming
And to reconcile the lost
To redeem the whole creation
You did not despise the cross

For even in Your suffering
You saw to the other side
Knowing this was our salvation
Jesus for our sake You died

VERSE 3:
And the morning that You rose
All of heaven held its breath
Till that stone was moved for good
For the Lamb had conquered death

And the dead rose from their tombs
And the angels stood in awe
For the souls of all who'd come
To the Father are restored

© 2019 Hillsong Music Publishing Australia & Fellow Ships Music/So Essential Tunes (admin at EssentialMusicPublishing.com)
CCLI: 7127647

PO Box 1195 Castle Hill NSW 1765
Ph: +61 2 8853 5284 Fx: +61 2 8846 4625
E-mail: publishing@hillsong.com

VERSE 4:
And the Church of Christ was born
Then the Spirit lit the flame
Now this gospel truth of old
Shall not kneel shall not faint

By His blood and in His Name
In His freedom I am free
For the love of Jesus Christ
Who has resurrected me

© 2019 Hillsong Music Publishing Australia & Fellow Ships Music/So Essential Tunes (admin at EssentialMusicPublishing.com)
CCLI: 7127647

PO Box 1195 Castle Hill NSW 1765
Ph: +61 2 8853 5284 Fx: +61 2 8846 4625
E-mail: publishing@hillsong.com

I WILL PRAISE YOU

Words and Music by
BEN FIELDING, JOEL HOUSTON,
MATT CROCKER & DYLAN THOMAS

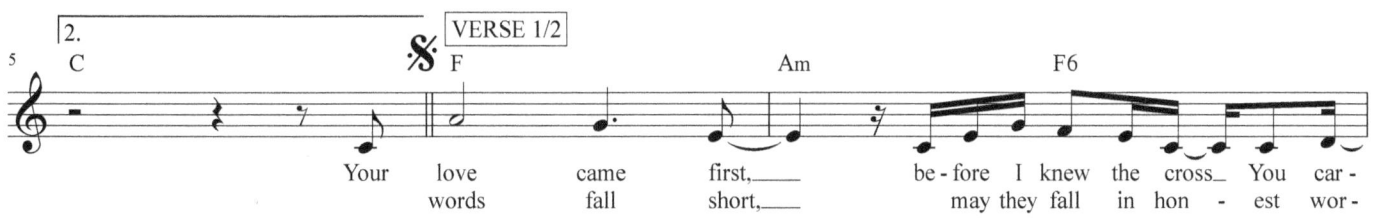

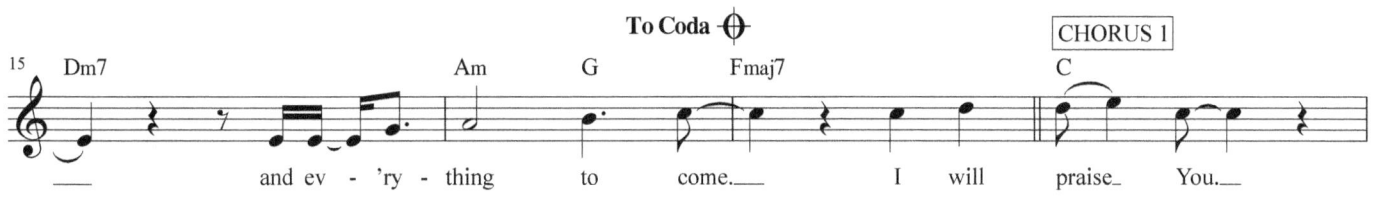
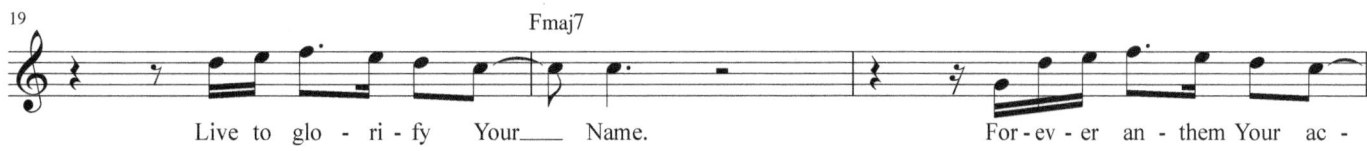

© 2019 Hillsong Music Publishing Australia.
All rights reserved. International copyright secured. Used by permission.
Tel: +61 2 8853 5284 Email: publishing@hillsong.com CCLI Song No. 7135002

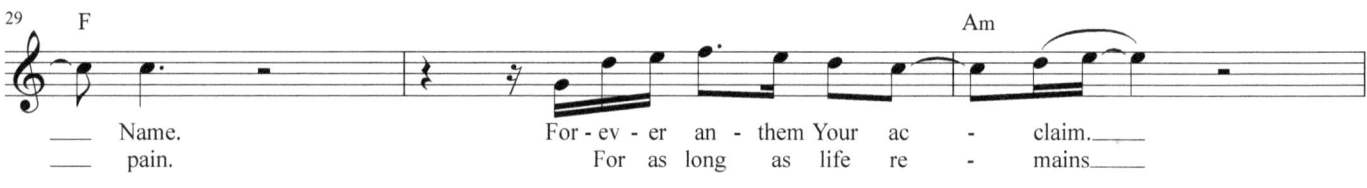
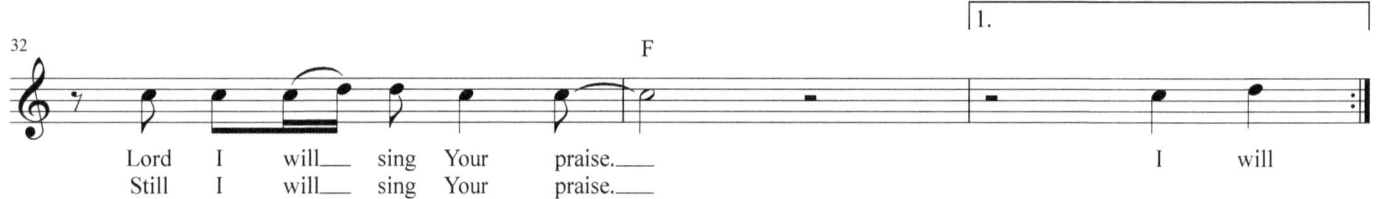

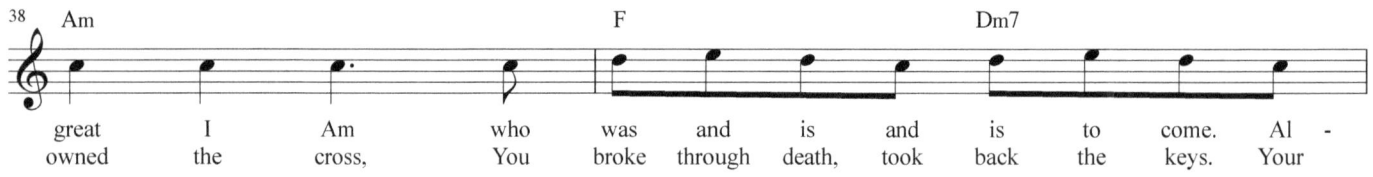
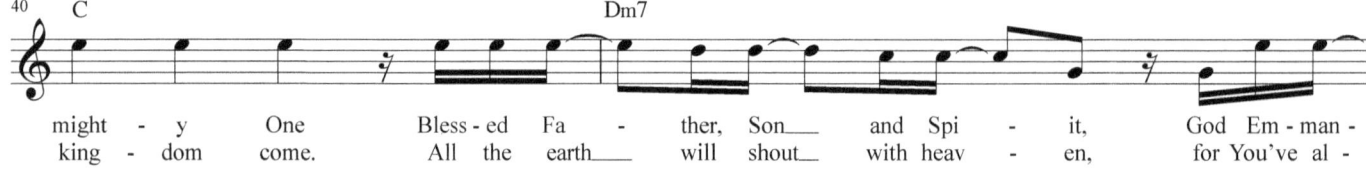

I WILL PRAISE YOU

**Words and Music By
Ben Fielding, Joel Houston,
Matt Crocker & Dylan Thomas**

VERSE 1:
Your love came first
Before I knew the cross You carried
Now free at last
I'll freely give as I've been given

PRE-CHORUS:
For everything You've done
And everything to come

CHORUS:
I will praise You
Live to glorify Your Name
Forever anthem Your acclaim
Lord I will sing Your praise

I will praise You
In the promise and the pain
For as long as life remains
Still I will sing Your praise

© 2019 Hillsong Music Publishing Australia
CCLI: 7135002

PO Box 1195 Castle Hill NSW 1765
Ph: +61 2 8853 5284 Fx: +61 2 8846 4625
E-mail: publishing@hillsong.com

VERSE 2:
Should words fall short
May they fall in honest worship
Till all I am
Breaks in reverence at Your feet

BRIDGE:
The first and last
The Alpha and Omega
God the great I Am
Who was and is and is to come
Almighty One
Blessed Father Son and Spirit
God Emmanuel is with us
Here and now and then forevermore

You rule in love
You reign in peace
You set me free
You owned the cross
You broke through death
Took back the keys
Your kingdom come

© 2019 Hillsong Music Publishing Australia
CCLI: 7135002

PO Box 1195 Castle Hill NSW 1765
Ph: +61 2 8853 5284 Fx: +61 2 8846 4625
E-mail: publishing@hillsong.com

All the earth will shout with heaven
For You've always held the glory
And You always will
Forever

© 2019 Hillsong Music Publishing Australia
CCLI: 7135002

PO Box 1195 Castle Hill NSW 1765
Ph: +61 2 8853 5284 Fx: +61 2 8846 4625
E-mail: publishing@hillsong.com

FROM WHOM ALL BLESSINGS FLOW (DOXOLOGY)

Words and Music by
CHRIS DAVENPORT, BROOKE LIGERTWOOD
& SCOTT LIGERTWOOD

Anthemically ♩ = 72

VERSE 1/2

What gift of love could I offer to a King?
A glory song is inscribed upon my heart.

Play cues on repeat

What weight or worth could be held within my offering? When
This treasure held in an alabaster jar, I break to

He alone is worthy.
bring Him all the glory.

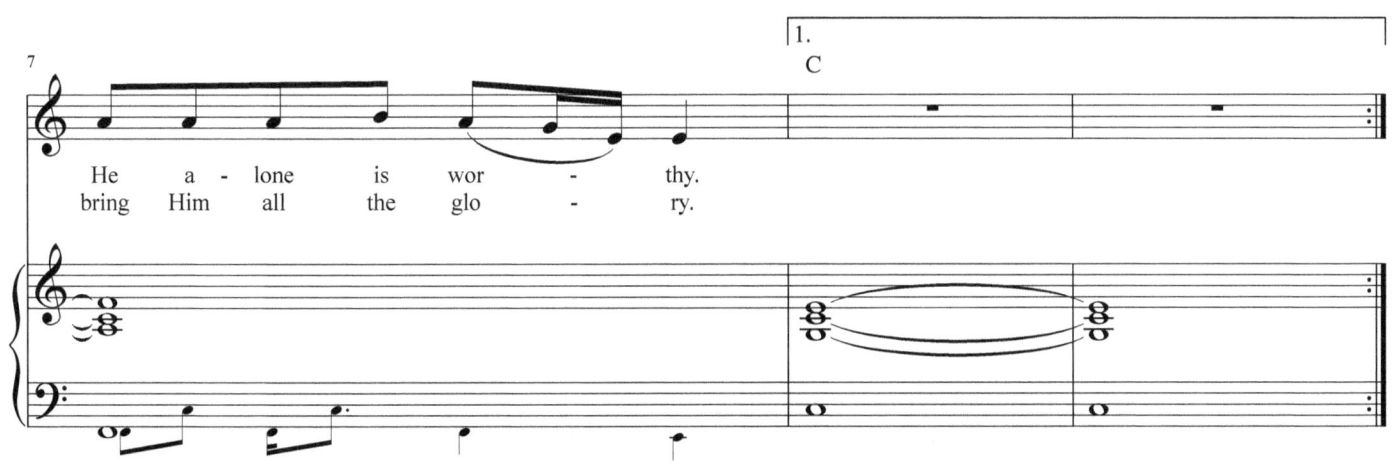

© 2019 Hillsong MP Songs (BMI) & Hillsong Music Publishing Australia.
All rights reserved. International copyright secured. Used by permission.
Tel: +61 2 8853 5284 Email: publishing@hillsong.com CCLI Song No. 7134995

FROM WHOM ALL BLESSINGS FLOW (DOXOLOGY)

Words and Music by
CHRIS DAVENPORT, BROOKE LIGERTWOOD
& SCOTT LIGERTWOOD

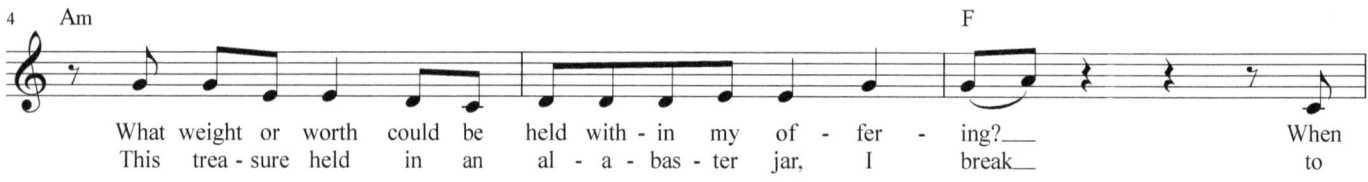
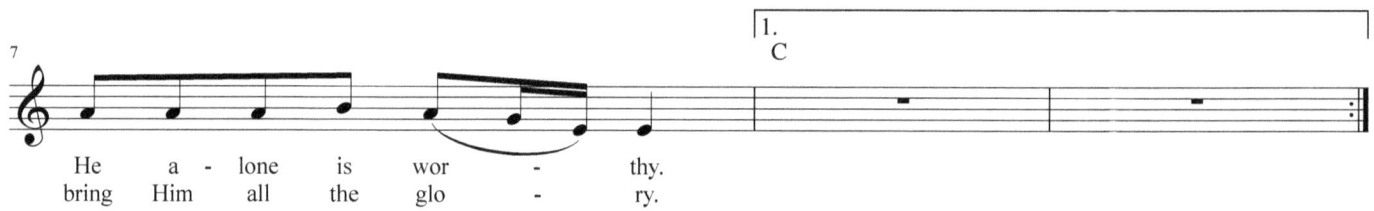

© 2019 Hillsong MP Songs (BMI) & Hillsong Music Publishing Australia.
All rights reserved. International copyright secured. Used by permission.
Tel: +61 2 8853 5284 Email: publishing@hillsong.com CCLI Song No. 7134995

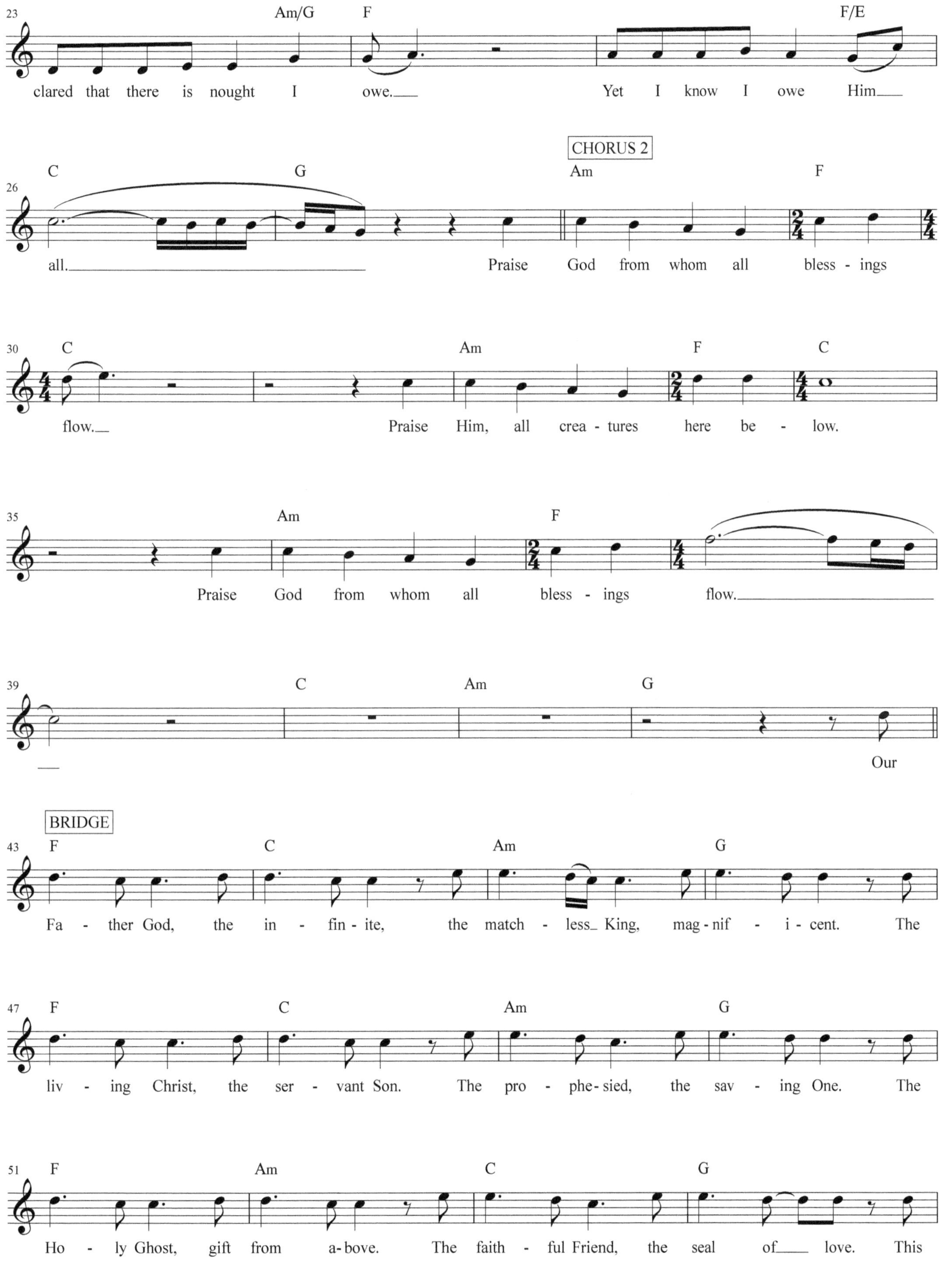
23 Am/G F F/E
clared that there is nought I owe.__ Yet I know I owe Him__
CHORUS 2
26 C G Am F
all.__ Praise God from whom all bless - ings
30 C Am F C
flow.__ Praise Him, all crea - tures here be - low.
35 Am F
Praise God from whom all bless - ings flow.__
39 C Am G
Our
BRIDGE
43 F C Am G
Fa - ther God, the in - fin - ite, the match - less_ King, mag - nif - i - cent. The
47 F C Am G
liv - ing Christ, the ser - vant Son. The pro - phe - sied, the sav - ing One. The
51 F Am C G
Ho - ly Ghost, gift from a - bove. The faith - ful Friend, the seal of__ love. This

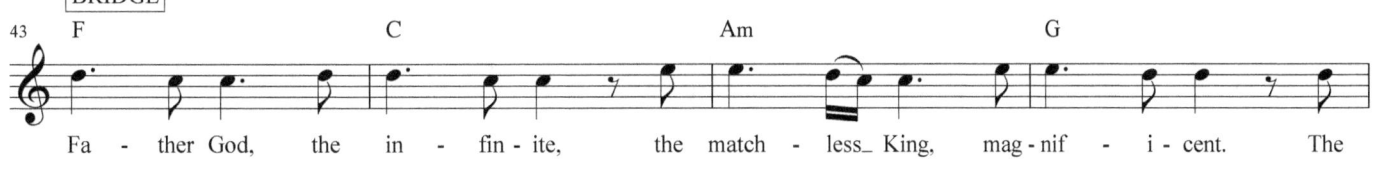

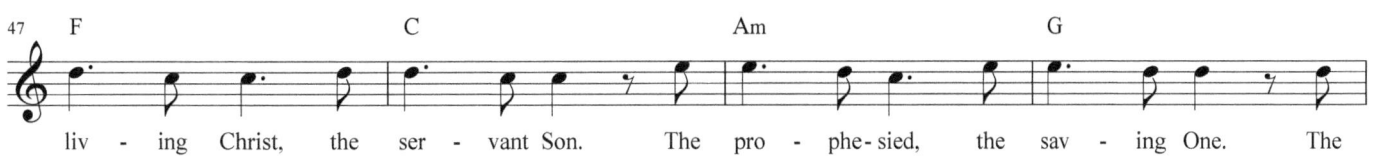

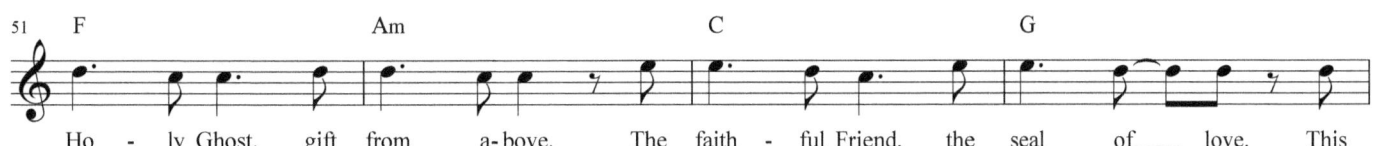

FROM WHOM ALL BLESSINGS FLOW (DOXOLOGY)

Words and Music by
Chris Davenport, Brooke Ligertwood
& Scott Ligertwood

VERSE 1:
What gift of love could I offer to a King
What weight or worth could be held within my offering
When He alone is worthy

VERSE 2:
A glory song is inscribed upon my heart
This treasure held in an alabaster jar I break
To bring Him all the glory

CHORUS:
Praise God from whom all blessings flow
Praise Him all creatures here below

© 2019 Hillsong MP Songs (BMI) & Hillsong Music Publishing Australia
CCLI: 7134995

PO Box 1195 Castle Hill NSW 1765
Ph: +61 2 8853 5284 Fx: +61 2 8846 4625
E-mail: publishing@hillsong.com

VERSE 3:
What sacrifice could be equal to His own
The cross of Christ has declared that there is nought I owe
Yet I know I owe Him all

CHORUS 2:
Praise God from whom all blessings flow
Praise Him all creatures here below
Praise God from whom all blessings flow

BRIDGE:
Our Father God the infinite
The matchless King magnificent

The living Christ the servant Son
The prophesied the saving One

The Holy Ghost gift from above
The faithful Friend the seal of love

This life this heart this song to Him
My all in all my everything

© 2019 Hillsong MP Songs (BMI) & Hillsong Music Publishing Australia
CCLI: 7134995

PO Box 1195 Castle Hill NSW 1765
Ph: +61 2 8853 5284 Fx: +61 2 8846 4625
E-mail: publishing@hillsong.com

CHORUS 3:
Praise God from whom all blessings flow
Praise Him all creatures here below
Praise Him above ye heavenly hosts
Praise Father Son and Holy Ghost

© 2019 Hillsong MP Songs (BMI) & Hillsong Music Publishing Australia
CCLI: 7134995

PO Box 1195 Castle Hill NSW 1765
Ph: +61 2 8853 5284 Fx: +61 2 8846 4625
E-mail: publishing@hillsong.com

EVERY BREATH

Words and Music by
HANNAH HOBBS & BEN TAN

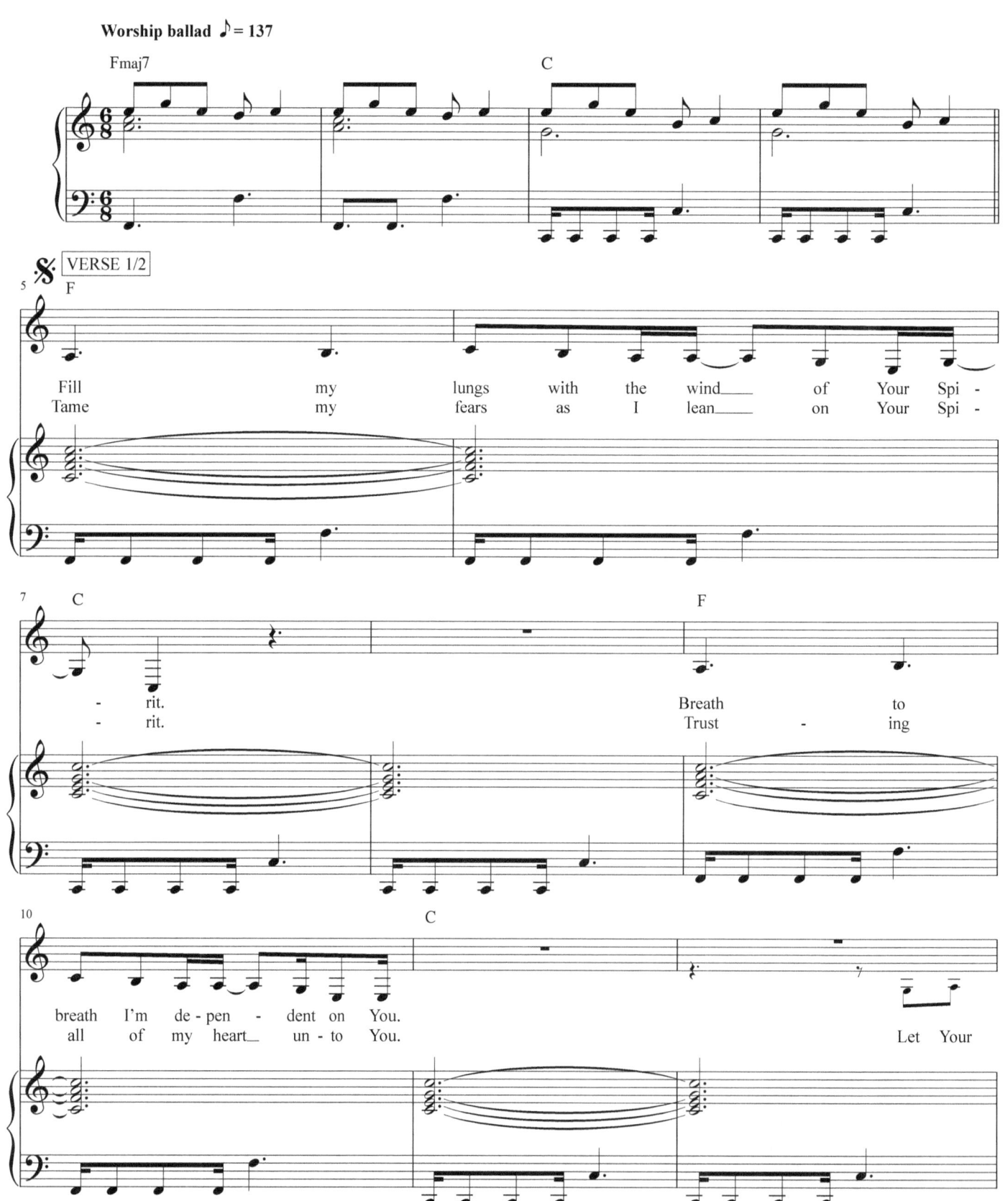

© 2019 Hillsong Music Publishing Australia.
All rights reserved. International copyright secured. Used by permission.
Tel: +61 2 8853 5284 Email: publishing@hillsong.com CCLI Song No. 7134999

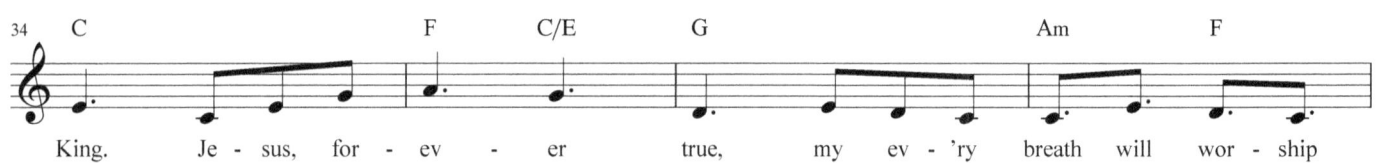
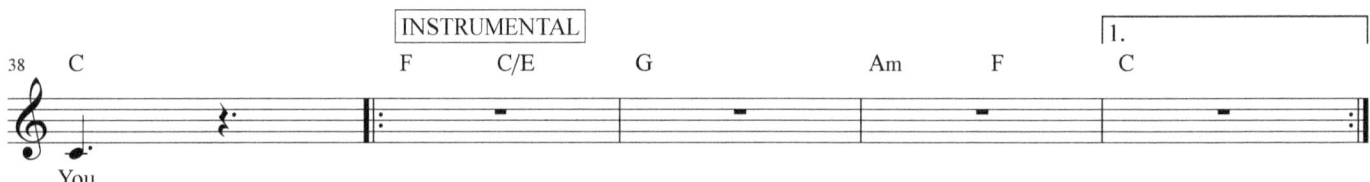
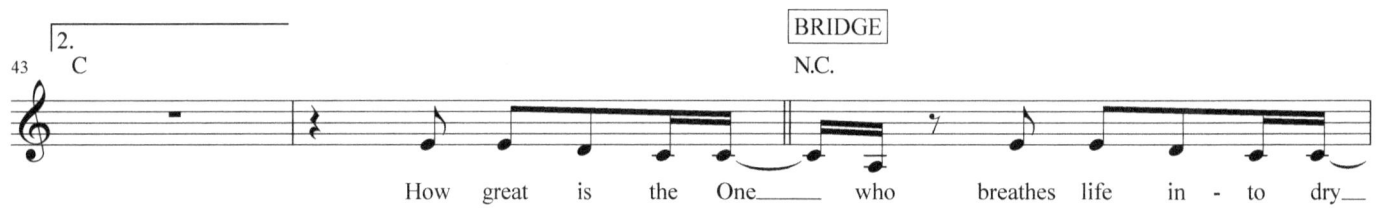

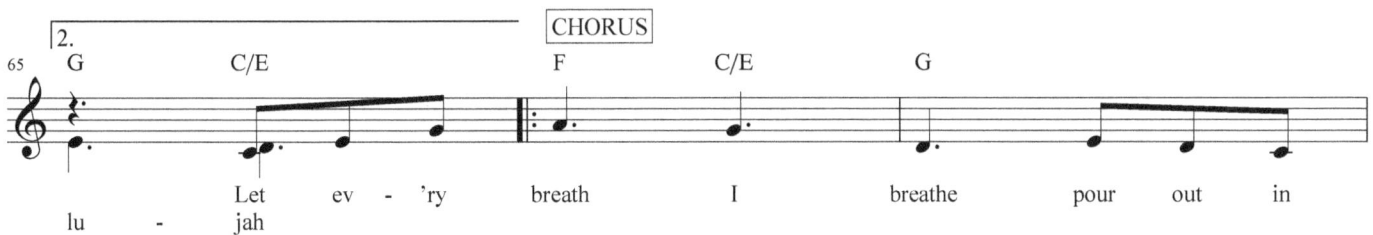
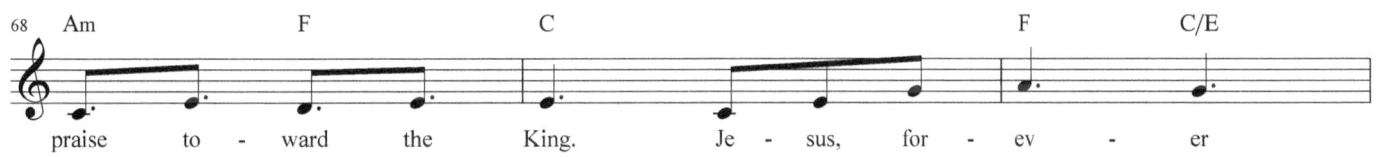

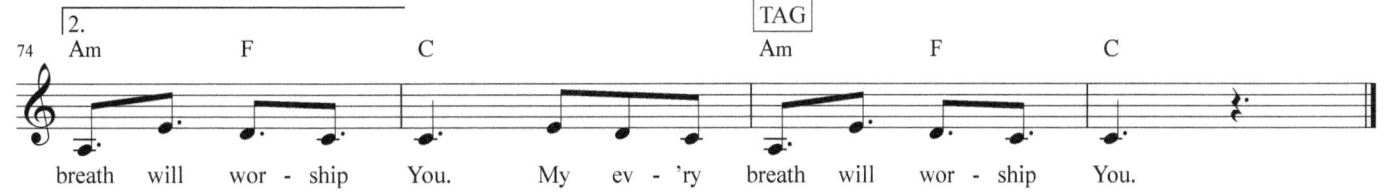

EVERY BREATH

**Words and Music by
Hannah Hobbs & Ben Tan**

VERSE 1:
Fill my lungs with the wind of Your Spirit
Breath to breath I'm dependent on You
Faithful God You are calling me closer

PRE-CHORUS:
When morning dawns
And evening fades
I need Your grace

CHORUS:
Let every breath I breathe
Pour out in praise toward the King
Jesus forever true
My every breath will worship You

VERSE 2:
Tame my fears as I lean on Your Spirit
Trusting all of my heart unto You
Let Your passion burn like a fire in my soul

© 2019 Hillsong Music Publishing Australia
CCLI: 7134999

PO Box 1195 Castle Hill NSW 1765
Ph: +61 2 8853 5284 Fx: +61 2 8846 4625
E-mail: publishing@hillsong.com

PRE-CHORUS 2:
When morning dawns
And evening fades
I'll seek Your face

BRIDGE:
How great is the One who breathes life into dry bones
Heaven exhales and my soul is revived

How great is the One whose hope lines the horizon
Just when it feels like the end there's new life

How great is the One who brushed death off our shoulders
Victory came when He took back the night

The heart of our Saviour deserving all praises
My hallelujah will echo through time

© 2019 Hillsong Music Publishing Australia
CCLI: 7134999

PO Box 1195 Castle Hill NSW 1765
Ph: +61 2 8853 5284 Fx: +61 2 8846 4625
E-mail: publishing@hillsong.com

Every Breath – Page 3

TAG:
Hallelujah
Hallelujah

© 2019 Hillsong Music Publishing Australia
CCLI: 7134999

PO Box 1195 Castle Hill NSW 1765
Ph: +61 2 8853 5284 Fx: +61 2 8846 4625
E-mail: publishing@hillsong.com

BRIGHT AS THE SUN

Words and Music by
JOEL HOUSTON

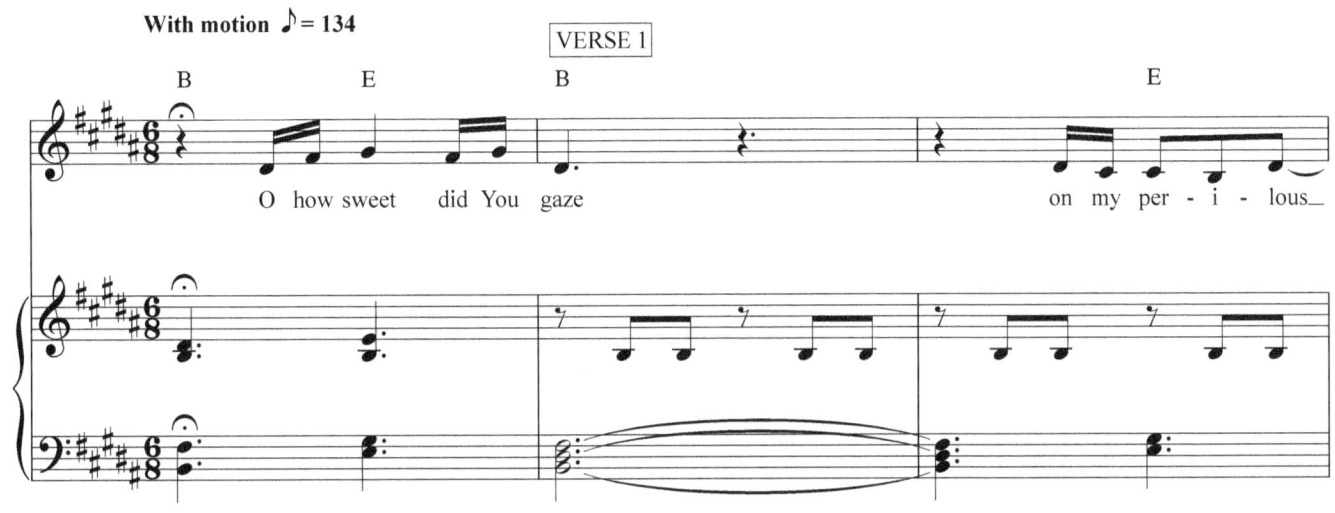

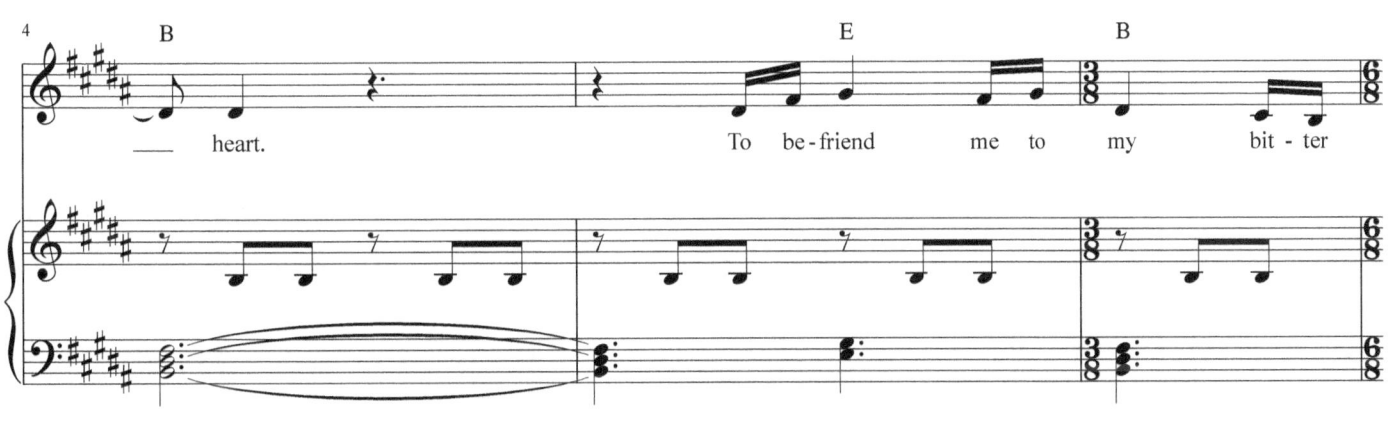

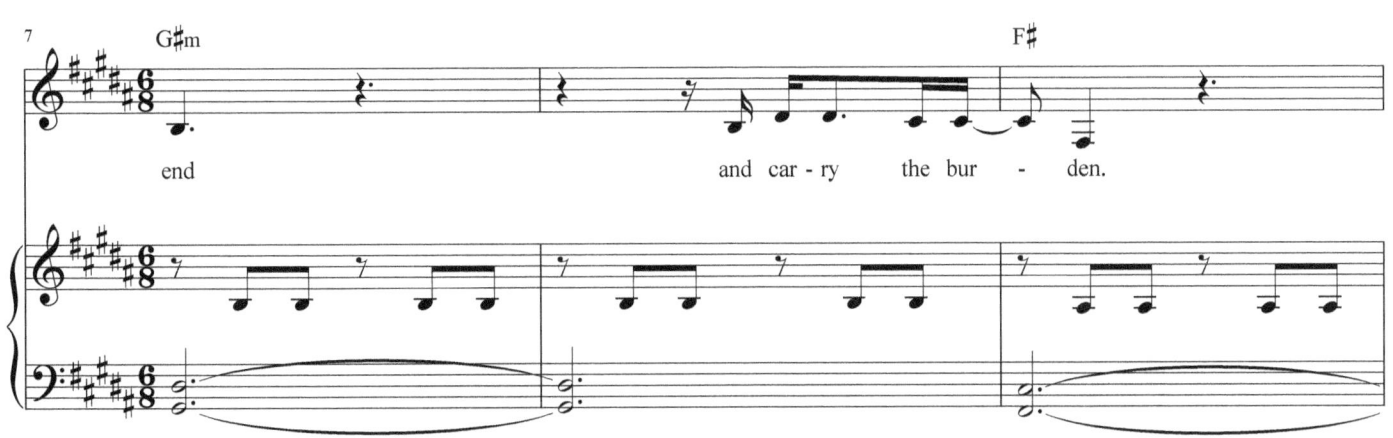

© 2019 Hillsong Music Publishing Australia.
All rights reserved. International copyright secured. Used by permission.
Tel: +61 2 8853 5284 Email: publishing@hillsong.com CCLI Song No. 7135001

BRIGHT AS THE SUN

Words and Music by
JOEL HOUSTON

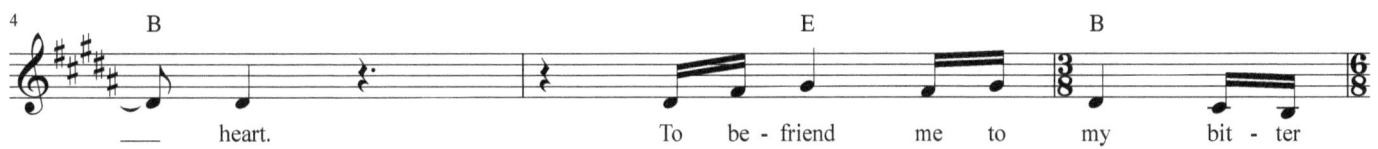

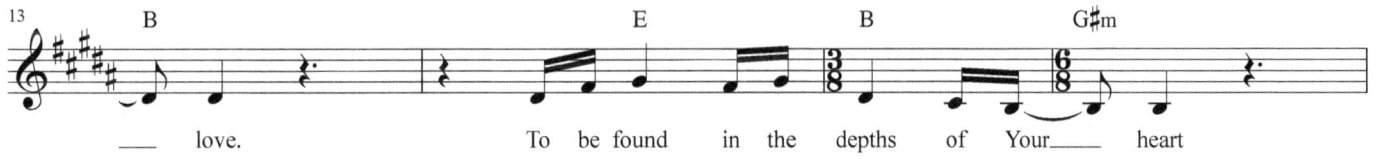

© 2019 Hillsong Music Publishing Australia.
All rights reserved. International copyright secured. Used by permission.
Tel: +61 2 8853 5284 Email: publishing@hillsong.com CCLI Song No. 7135001

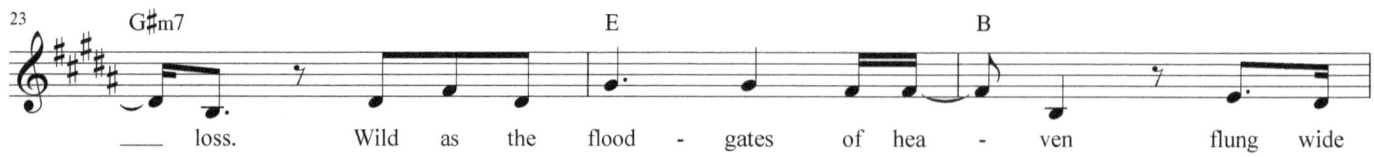
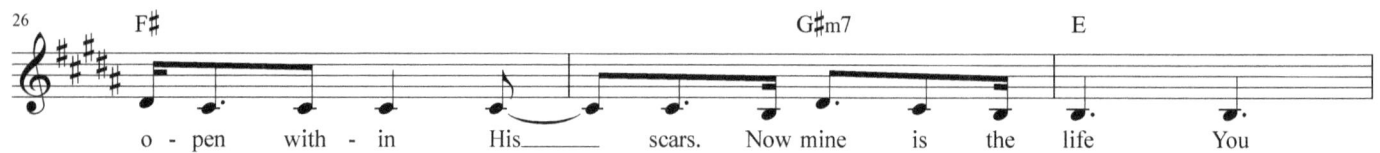
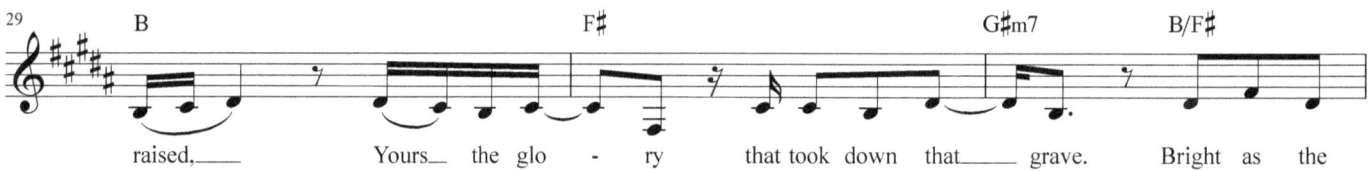

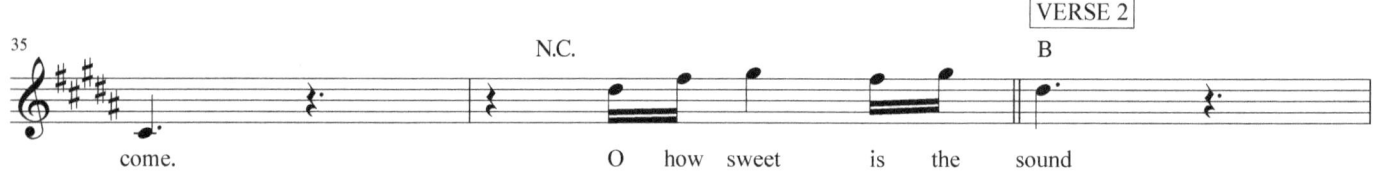
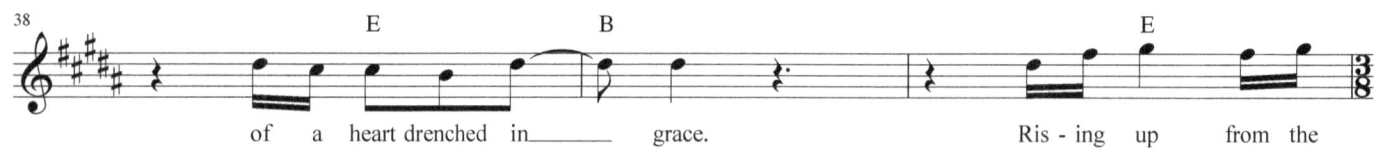

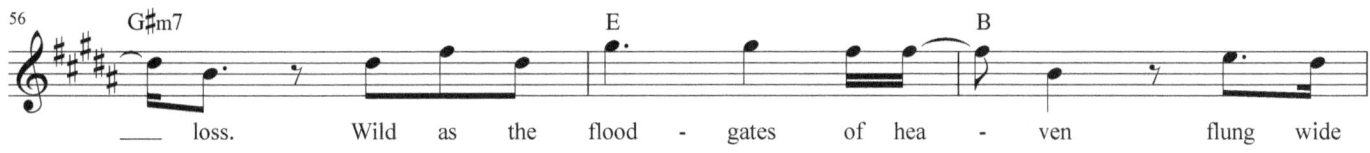

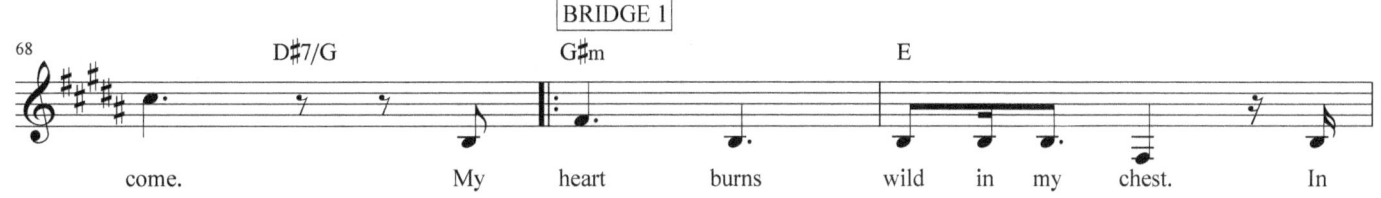

BRIGHT AS THE SUN

**Words and Music by
Joel Houston**

VERSE 1:
O how sweet did You gaze
On my perilous heart
To befriend me to my bitter end
And carry the burden

For as graven my failure
You prevailed in pure love
To be found in the depths of Your heart
As good as forgiven

© 2019 Hillsong Music Publishing Australia
CCLI: 7135001

PO Box 1195 Castle Hill NSW 1765
Ph: +61 2 8853 5284 Fx: +61 2 8846 4625
E-mail: publishing@hillsong.com

CHORUS:
O how You graced that cross
Where Jesus died and death took the loss
Wild as the floodgates of heaven
Flung wide open within His scars

Now mine is the life You raised
Yours the glory that took down that grave
Bright as the sun almighty in love
God forever Your Kingdom come

VERSE 2:
O how sweet is the sound
Of a heart drenched in grace
Rising up from the ashes in praise
Alive to Your greatness

Hope as brazen as mercy
Through the terrible night
How You blaze through the darkness I fight
Bright as the morning

© 2019 Hillsong Music Publishing Australia
CCLI: 7135001

PO Box 1195 Castle Hill NSW 1765
Ph: +61 2 8853 5284 Fx: +61 2 8846 4625
E-mail: publishing@hillsong.com

BRIDGE:
My heart burns wild in my chest
In awe of Your heart in all that You are
Let Your praise run wild on my breath
In awe of Your heart I'll sing it again

Till my heart beats out of my chest
I'll sing of Your love in awe of Your heart
Till Your praise is all I have left
I'll sing of Your love again and again

OUTRO:
Bright as the sun
Let us see Your Kingdom come
Bright as the sun
Have Your way Your Kingdom come

© 2019 Hillsong Music Publishing Australia
CCLI: 7135001

PO Box 1195 Castle Hill NSW 1765
Ph: +61 2 8853 5284 Fx: +61 2 8846 4625
E-mail: publishing@hillsong.com

UPPER ROOM

Words and Music by
BENJAMIN HASTINGS
& JOEL HOUSTON

© 2019 Hillsong Music Publishing Australia.
All rights reserved. International copyright secured. Used by permission.
Tel: +61 2 8853 5284 Email: publishing@hillsong.com CCLI Song No. 7134994

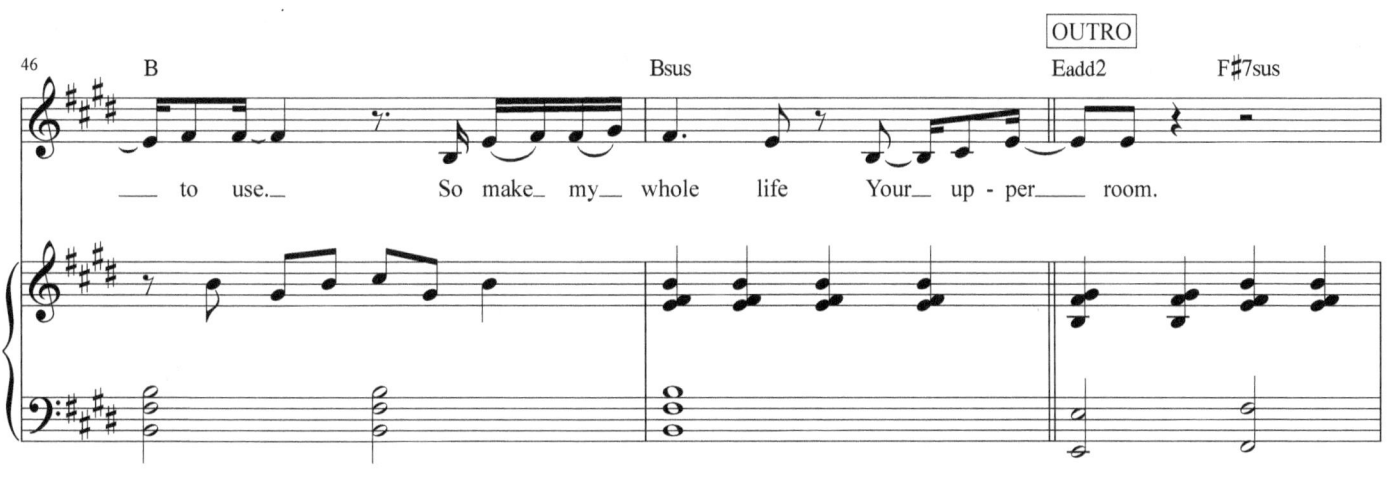
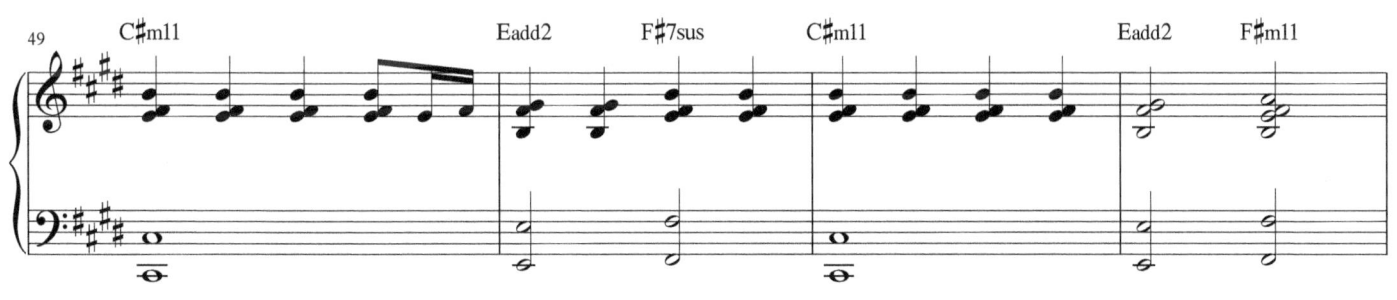
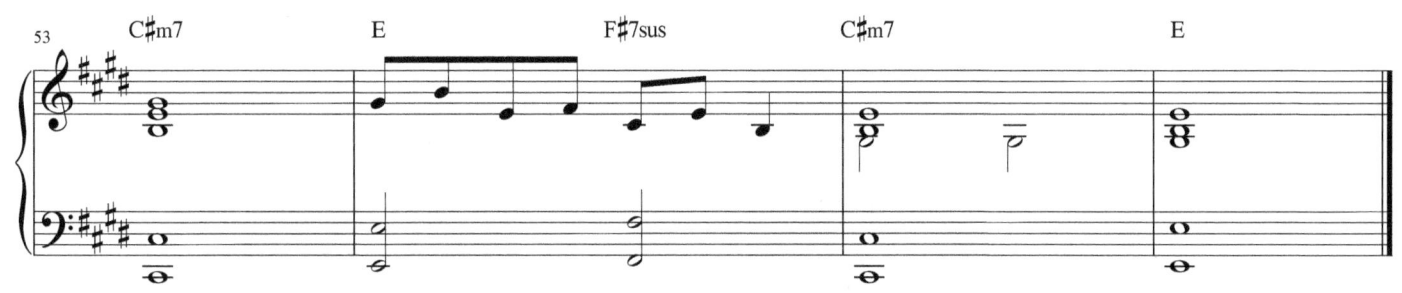

UPPER ROOM

**Words and Music by
BENJAMIN HASTINGS
& JOEL HOUSTON**

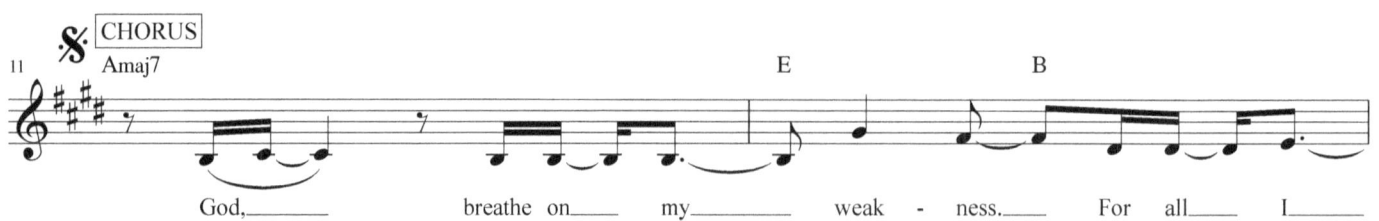

© 2019 Hillsong Music Publishing Australia.
All rights reserved. International copyright secured. Used by permission.
Tel: +61 2 8853 5284 Email: publishing@hillsong.com CCLI Song No. 7134994

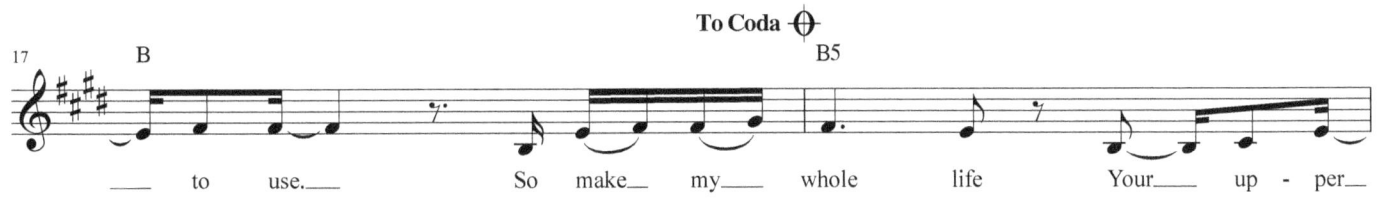

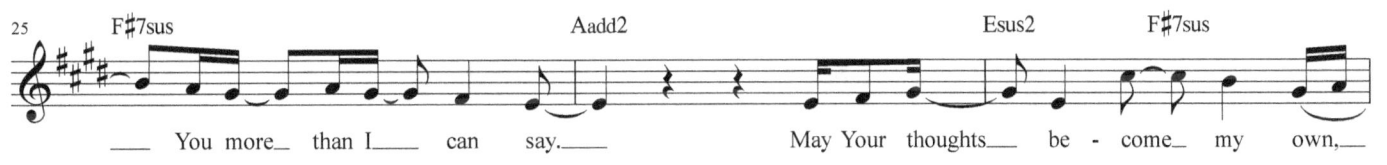

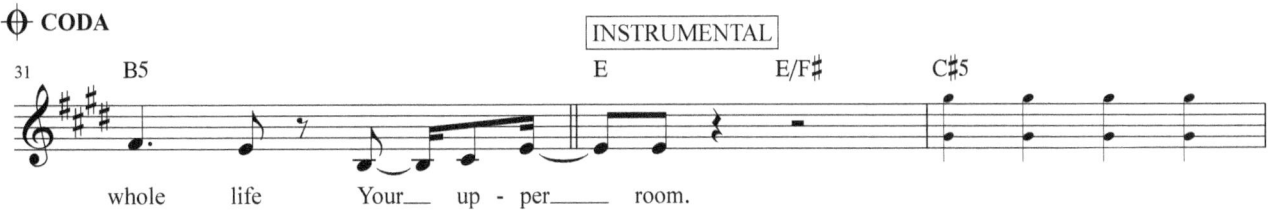

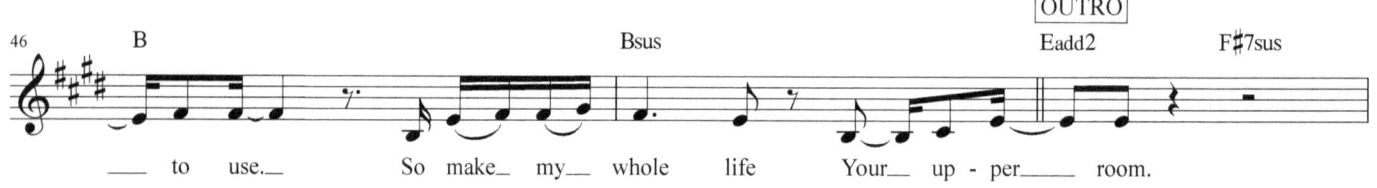

UPPER ROOM

**Words and Music by
Benjamin Hastings & Joel Houston**

VERSE 1:

Help me Holy Ghost
I need You more than anything
All my best ideas are Yours
What am I but what You make of me

CHORUS:

So help me God breathe on my weakness
For all I want is to be like Jesus
I don't have much
But what I have is Yours to use
So make my whole life Your upper room

VERSE 2:

Help me Holy Ghost
I need You more than I can say
May Your thoughts become my own
Till the Father's will be done in me

© 2019 Hillsong Music Publishing Australia
CCLI: 7134994

PO Box 1195 Castle Hill NSW 1765
Ph: +61 2 8853 5284 Fx: +61 2 8846 4625
E-mail: publishing@hillsong.com

HE SHALL REIGN

**Words and Music by
BEN FIELDING &
REUBEN MORGAN**

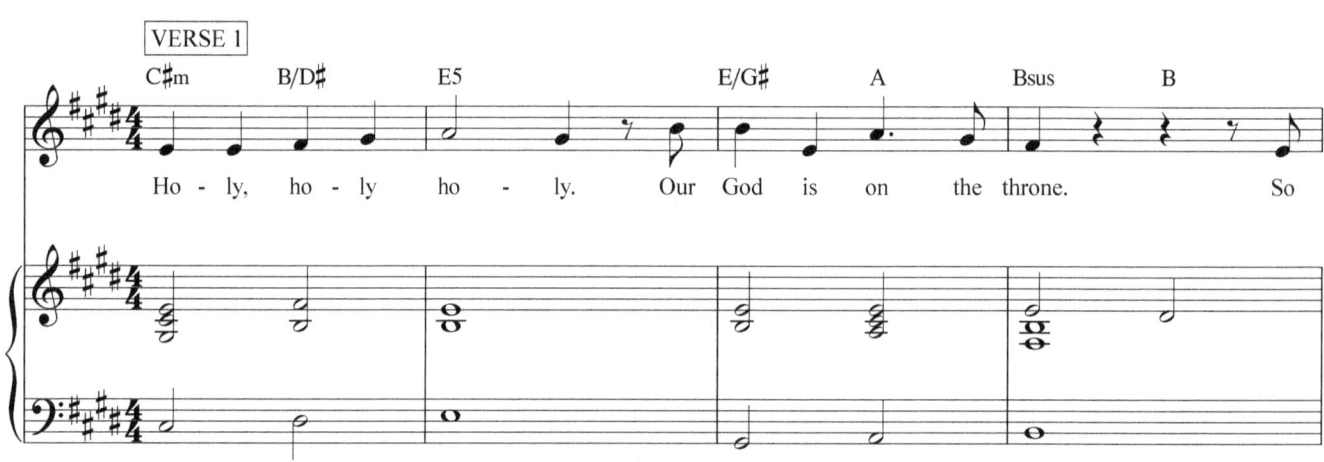

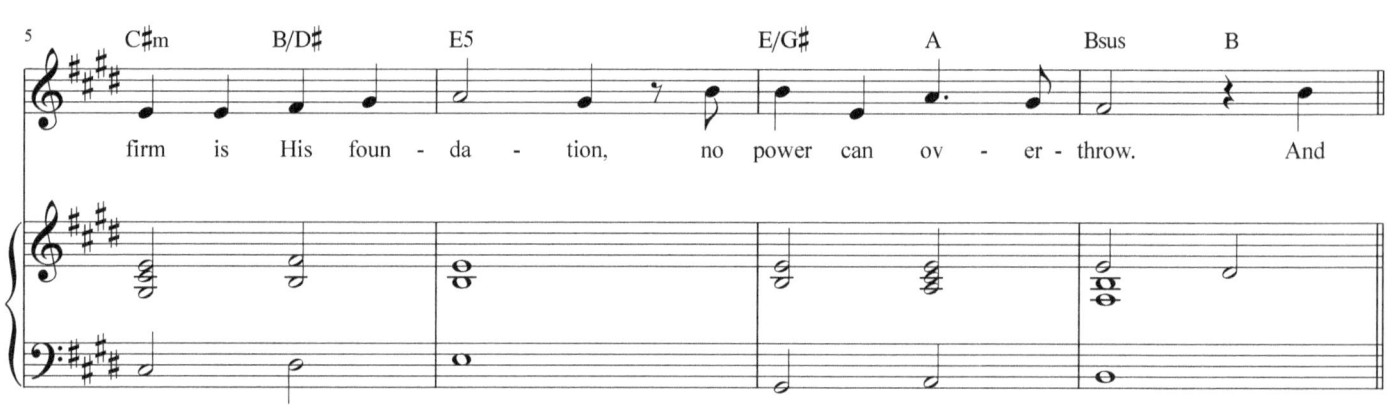

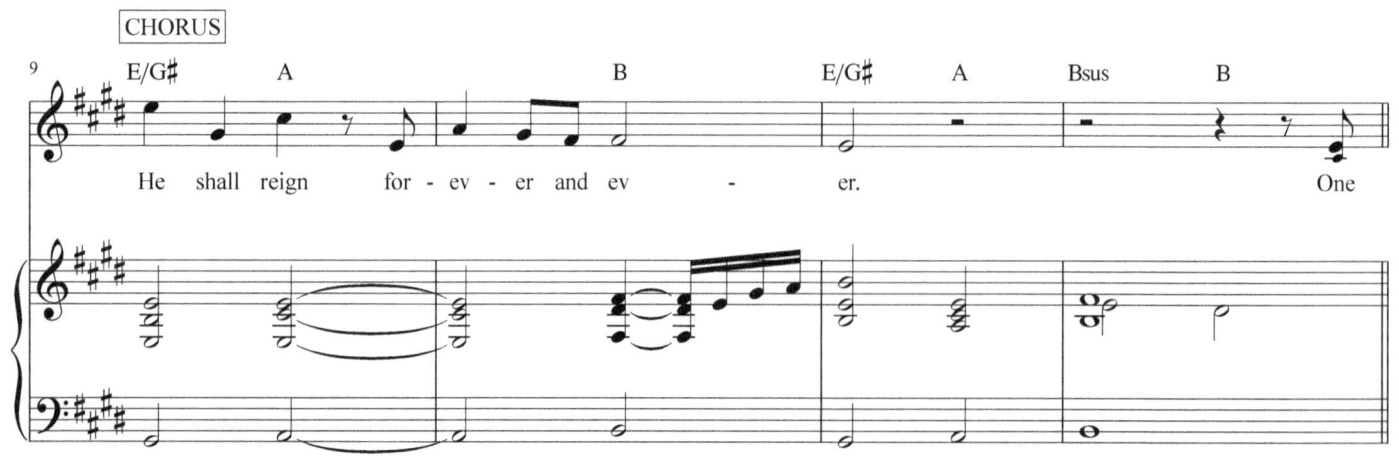

© 2019 Hillsong Music Publishing Australia.
All rights reserved. International copyright secured. Used by permission.
Tel: +61 2 8853 5284 Email: publishing@hillsong.com CCLI Song No. 7134997

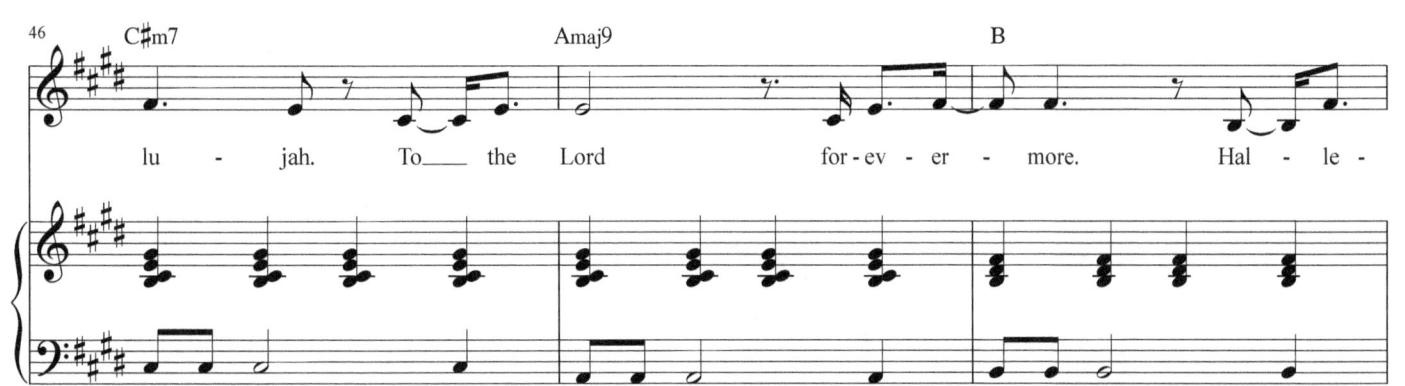

153

HE SHALL REIGN

Words and Music by
BEN FIELDING &
REUBEN MORGAN

© 2019 Hillsong Music Publishing Australia.
All rights reserved. International copyright secured. Used by permission.
Tel: +61 2 8853 5284 Email: publishing@hillsong.com CCLI Song No. 7134997

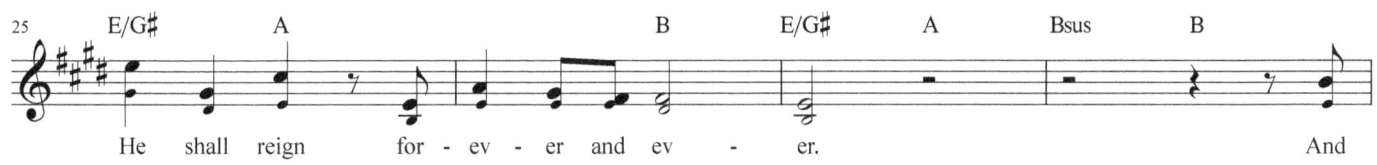

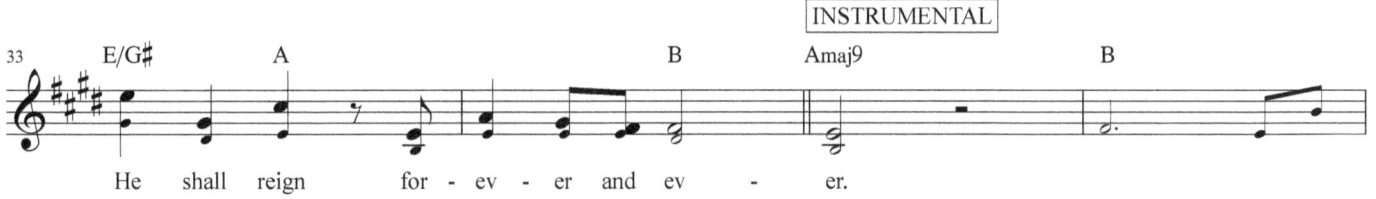

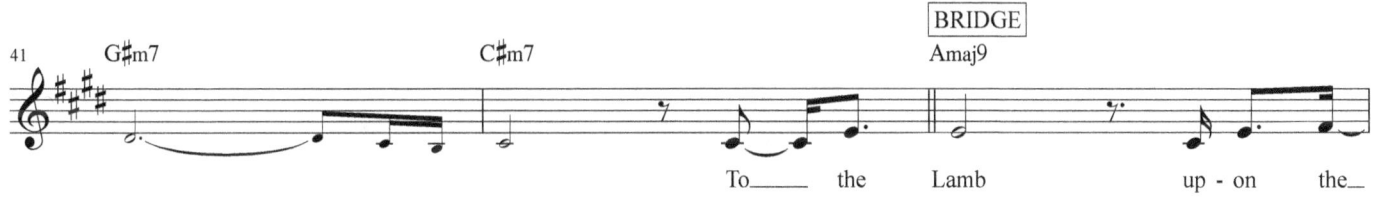

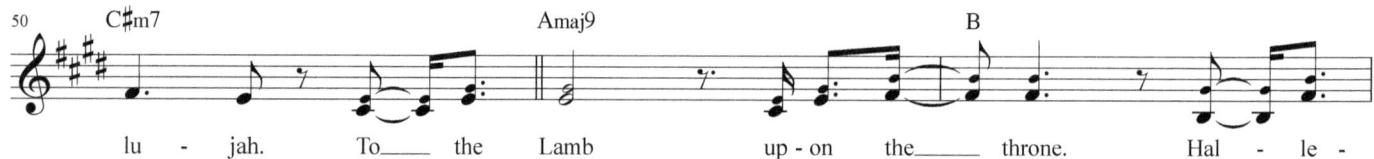

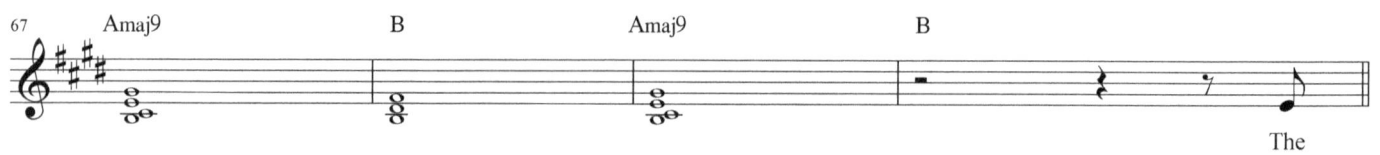

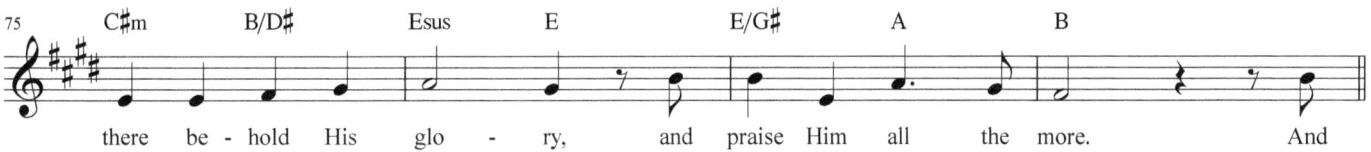

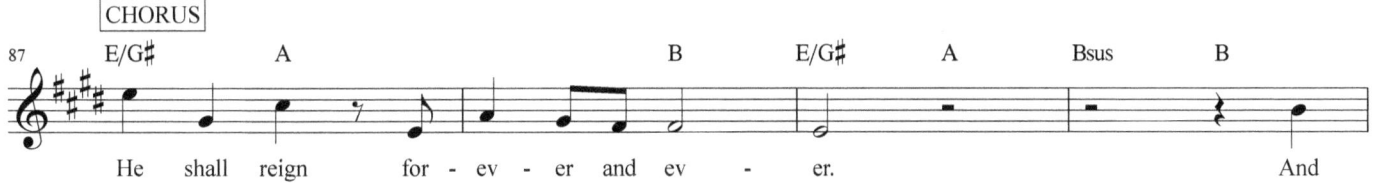
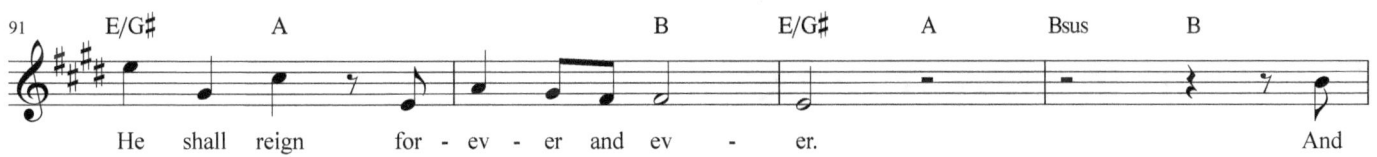
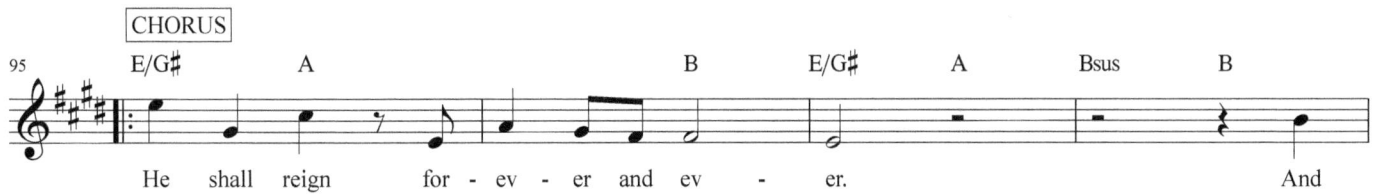
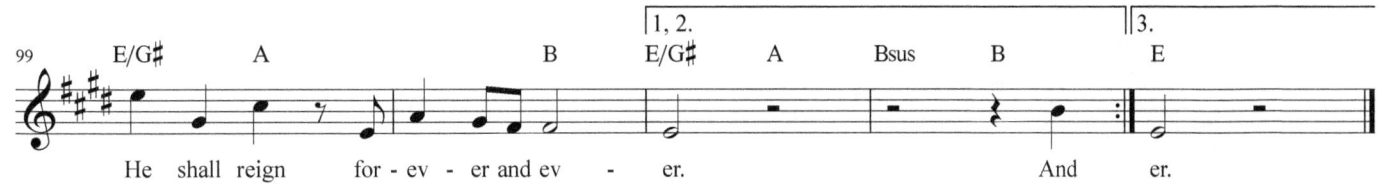

HE SHALL REIGN

**Words and Music by
Ben Fielding & Reuben Morgan**

VERSE 1:
Holy holy holy
Our God is on the throne
So firm is His foundation
No power can overthrow

CHORUS:
And He shall reign
Forever and ever

VERSE 2:
One Name outlasts the ages
Through time His truth revealed
While kings may pass like shadows
Our God is sovereign still

© 2019 Hillsong Music Publishing Australia
CCLI: 7134997

PO Box 1195 Castle Hill NSW 1765
Ph: +61 2 8853 5284 Fx: +61 2 8846 4625
E-mail: publishing@hillsong.com

BRIDGE:
To the Lamb upon the throne
Hallelujah hallelujah
To the Lord forevermore
Hallelujah hallelujah

Hallelujah hallelujah

VERSE 3:
The day I stand before Him
What praise will fill my soul
And there behold His glory
And praise Him all the more

© 2019 Hillsong Music Publishing Australia
CCLI: 7134997

PO Box 1195 Castle Hill NSW 1765
Ph: +61 2 8853 5284 Fx: +61 2 8846 4625
E-mail: publishing@hillsong.com

AWAKE

ALSO AVAILABLE IN THE FOLLOWING FORMATS:

CD

VINYL

DIGITAL WORSHIP KIT

HILLSONG.COM/WORSHIP

www.ingramcontent.com/pod-product-compliance
Lightning Source LLC
Chambersburg PA
CBHW080807300426
44114CB00020B/2856